DYLANNA PRESS

MUSIC

COLORING BOOK FOR ADULTS

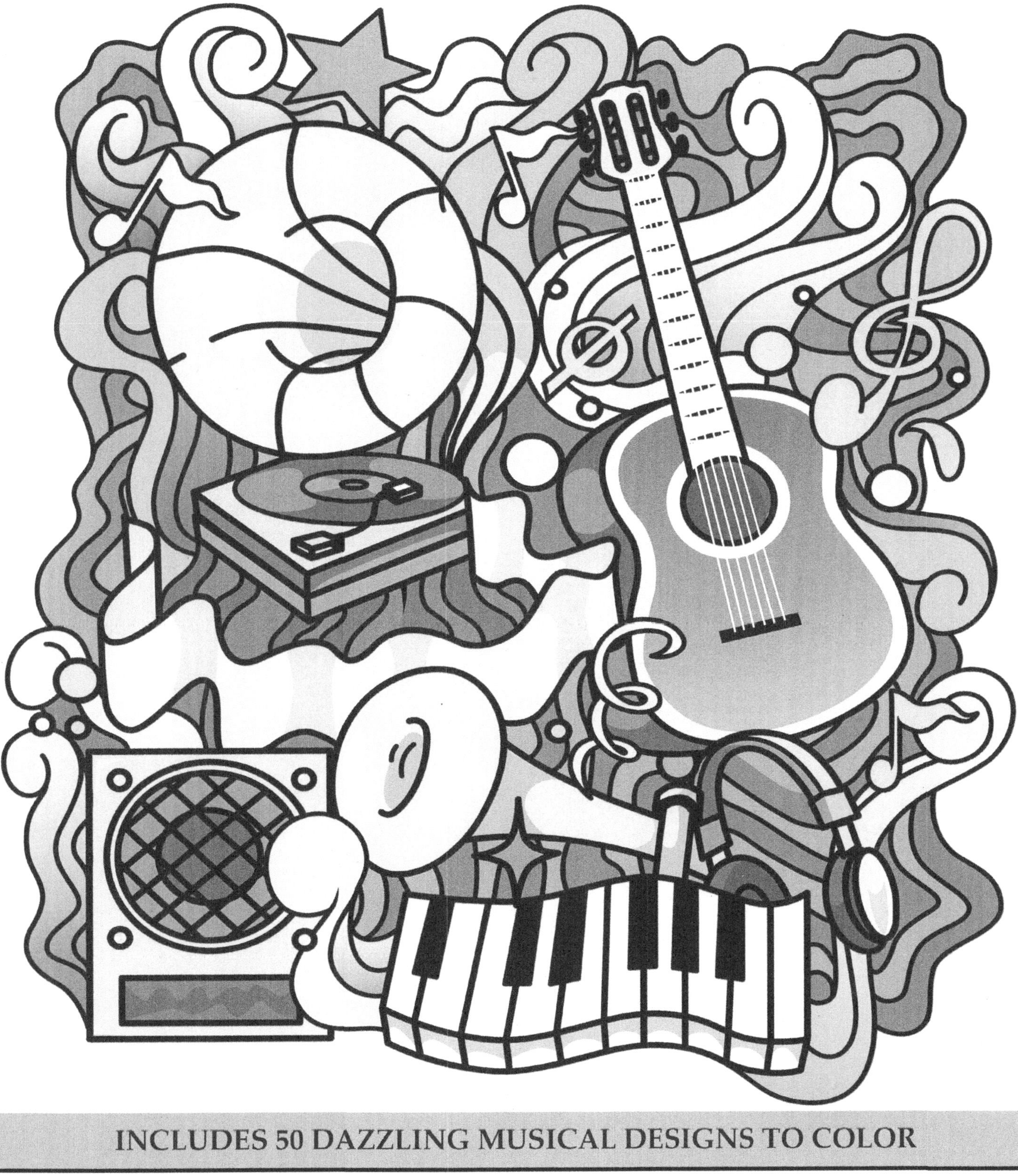

INCLUDES 50 DAZZLING MUSICAL DESIGNS TO COLOR

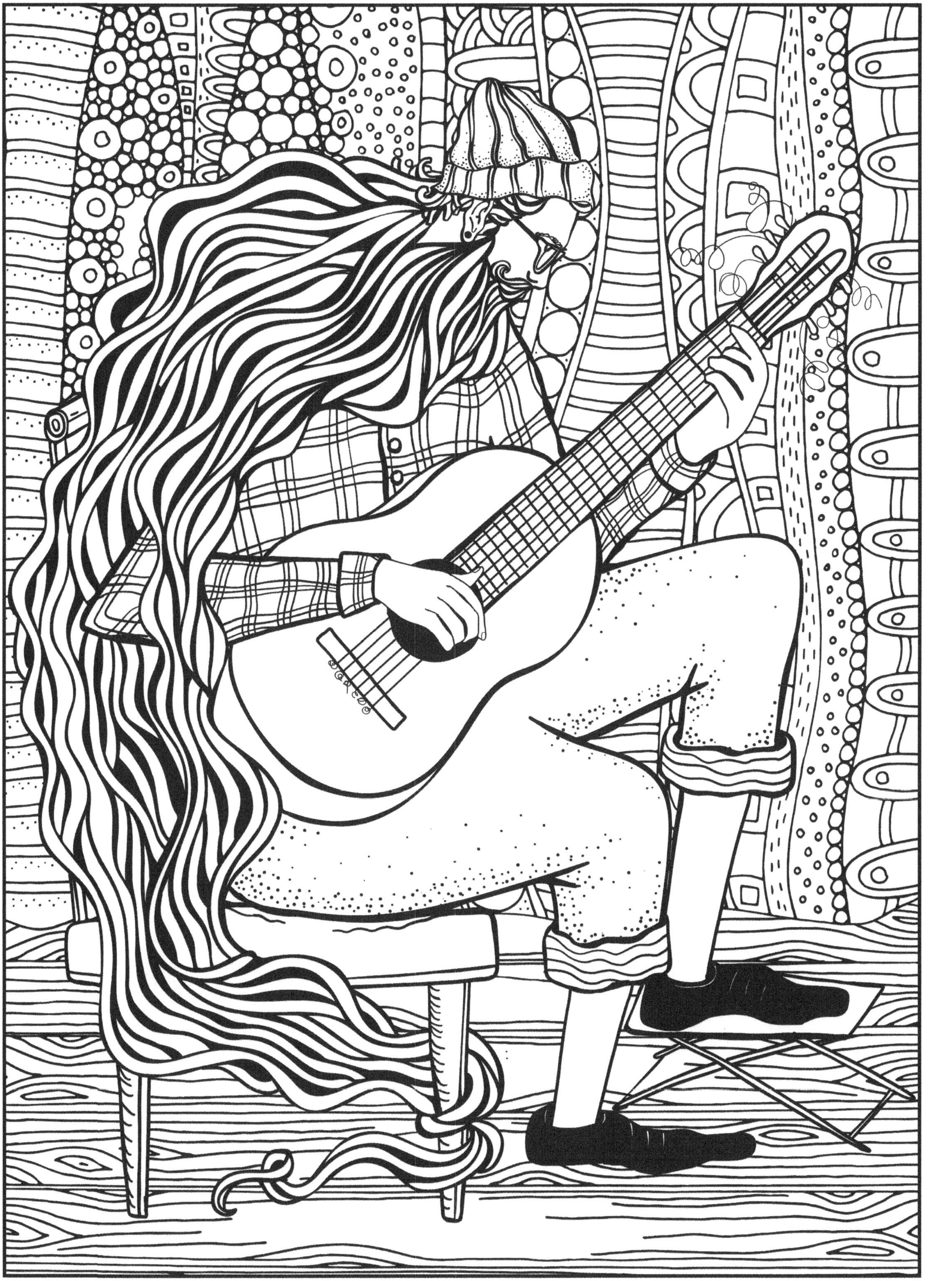

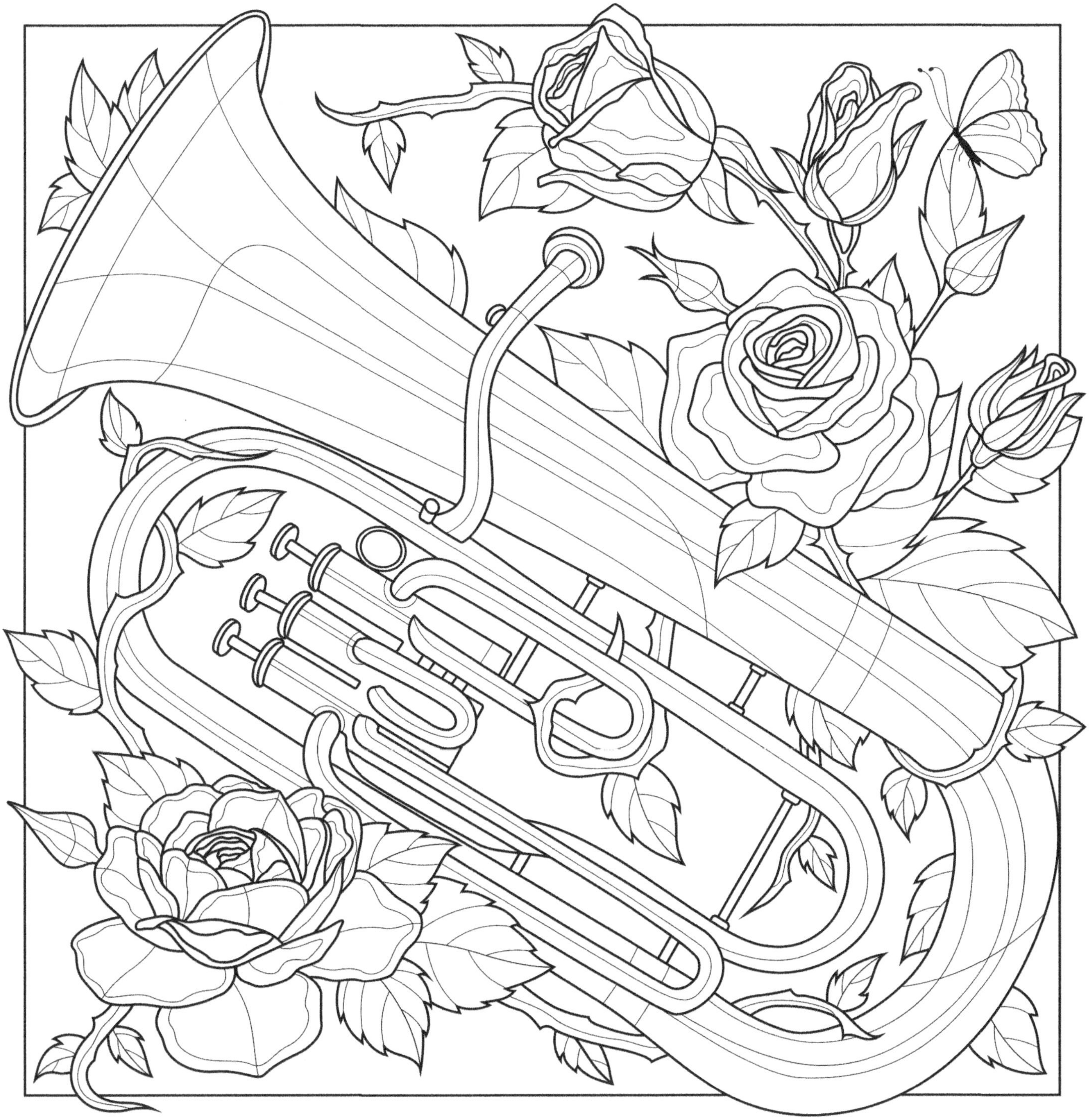

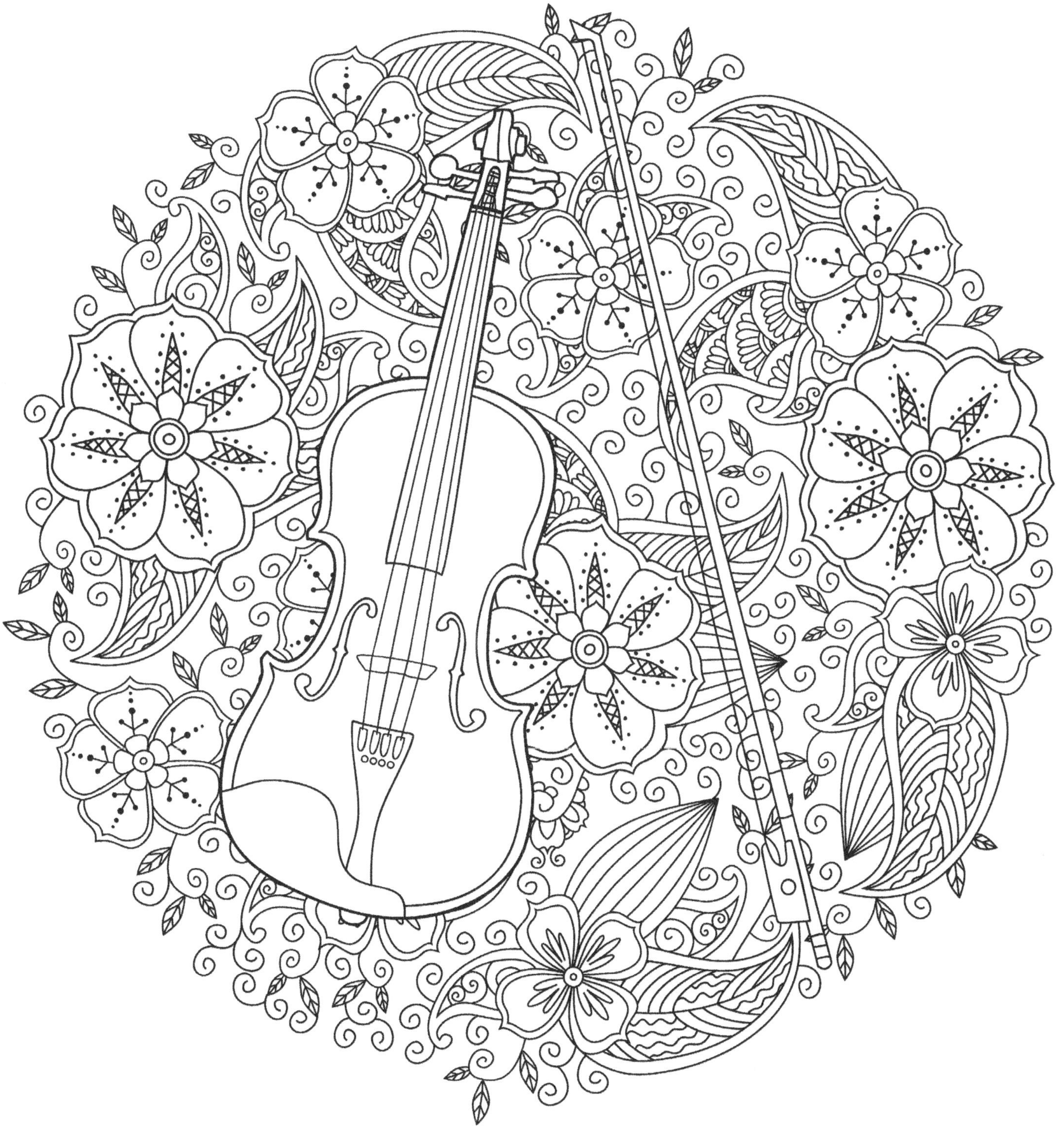

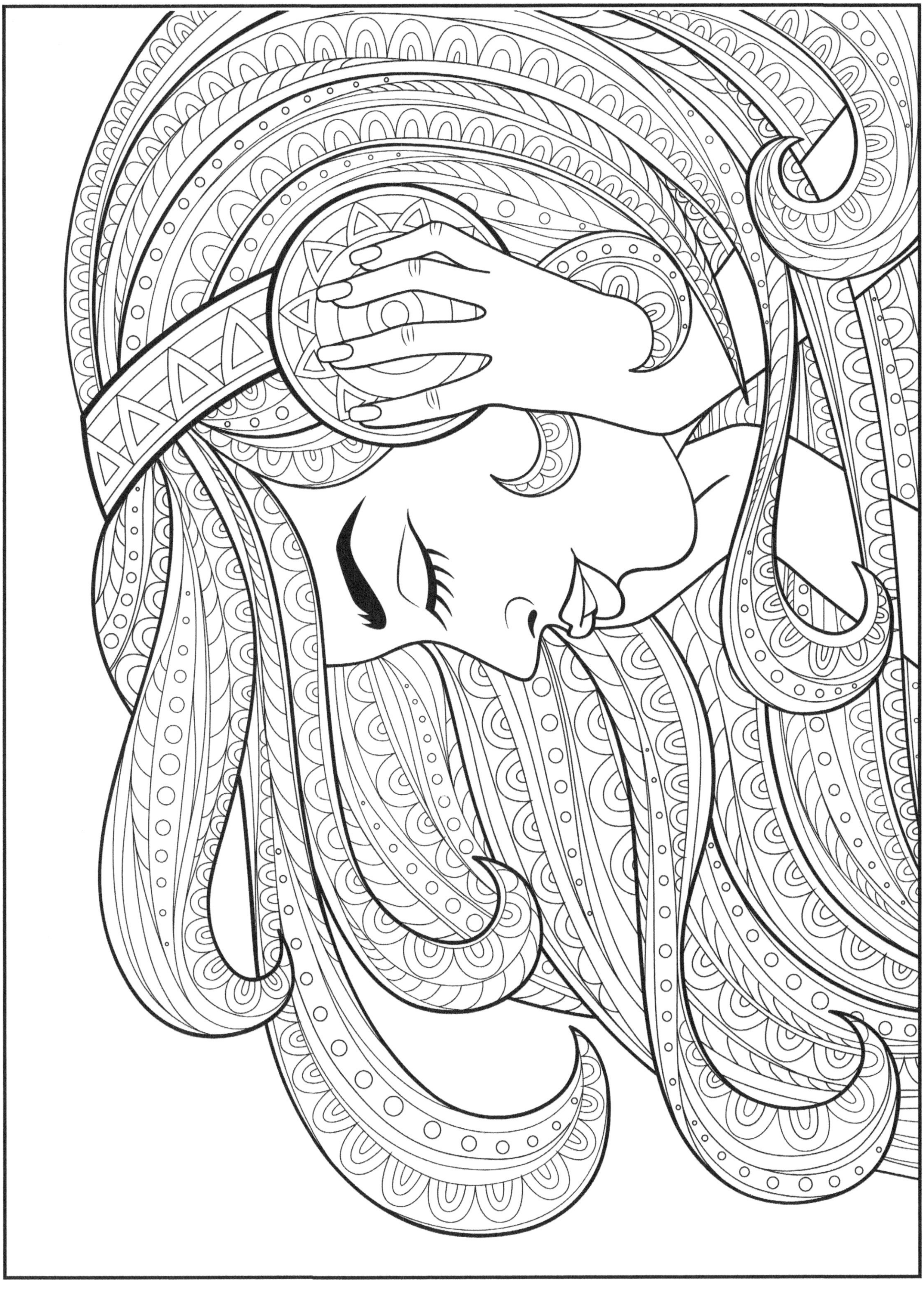

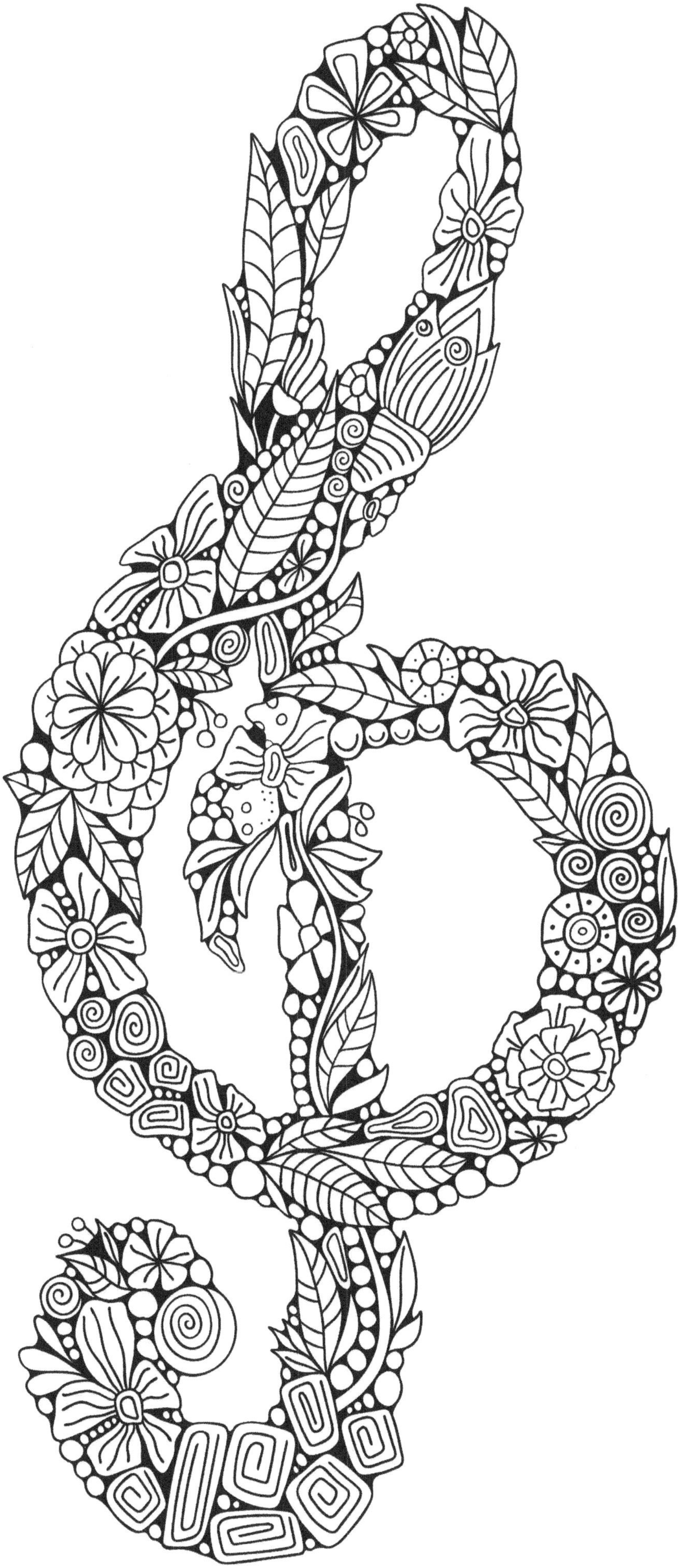

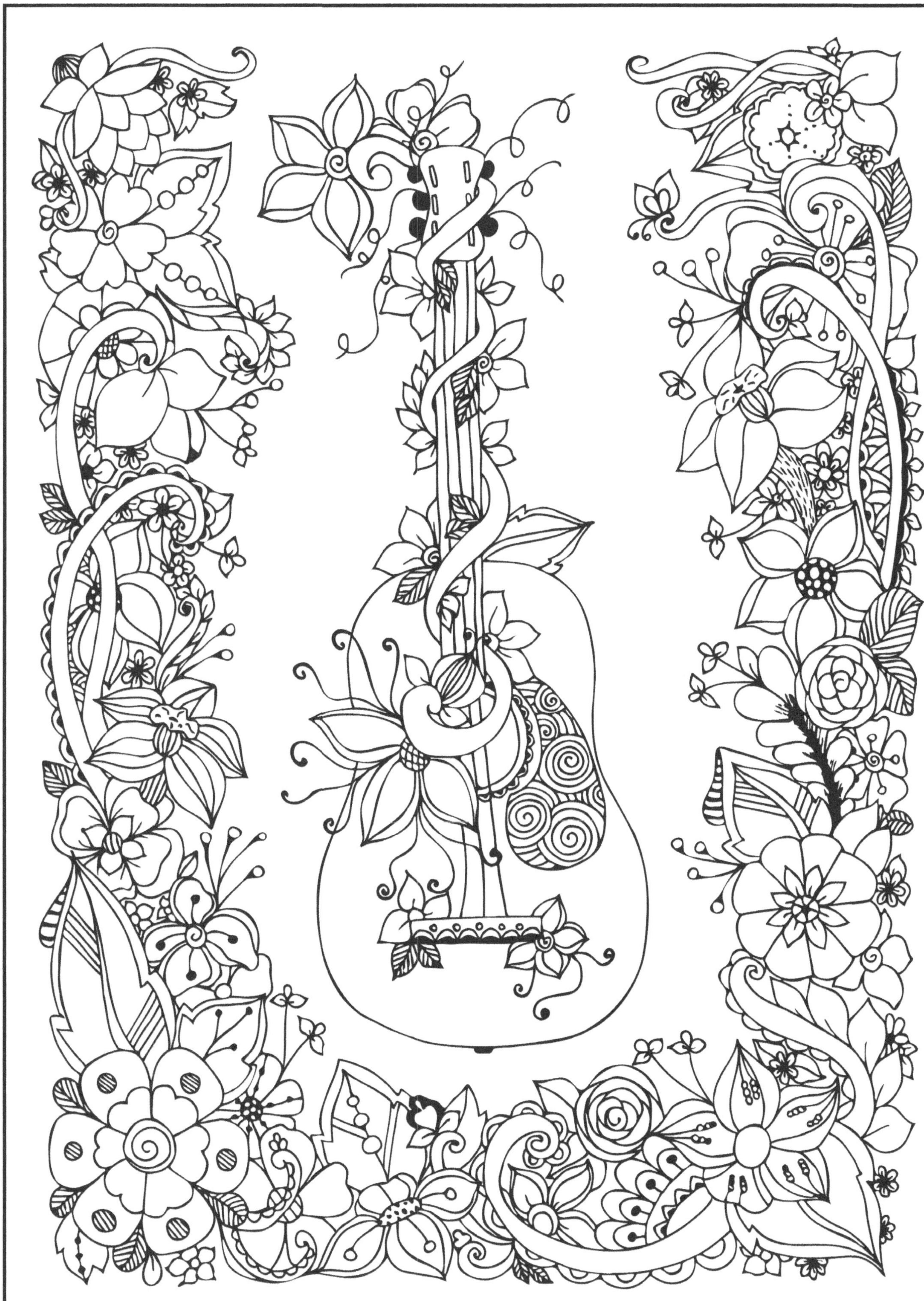

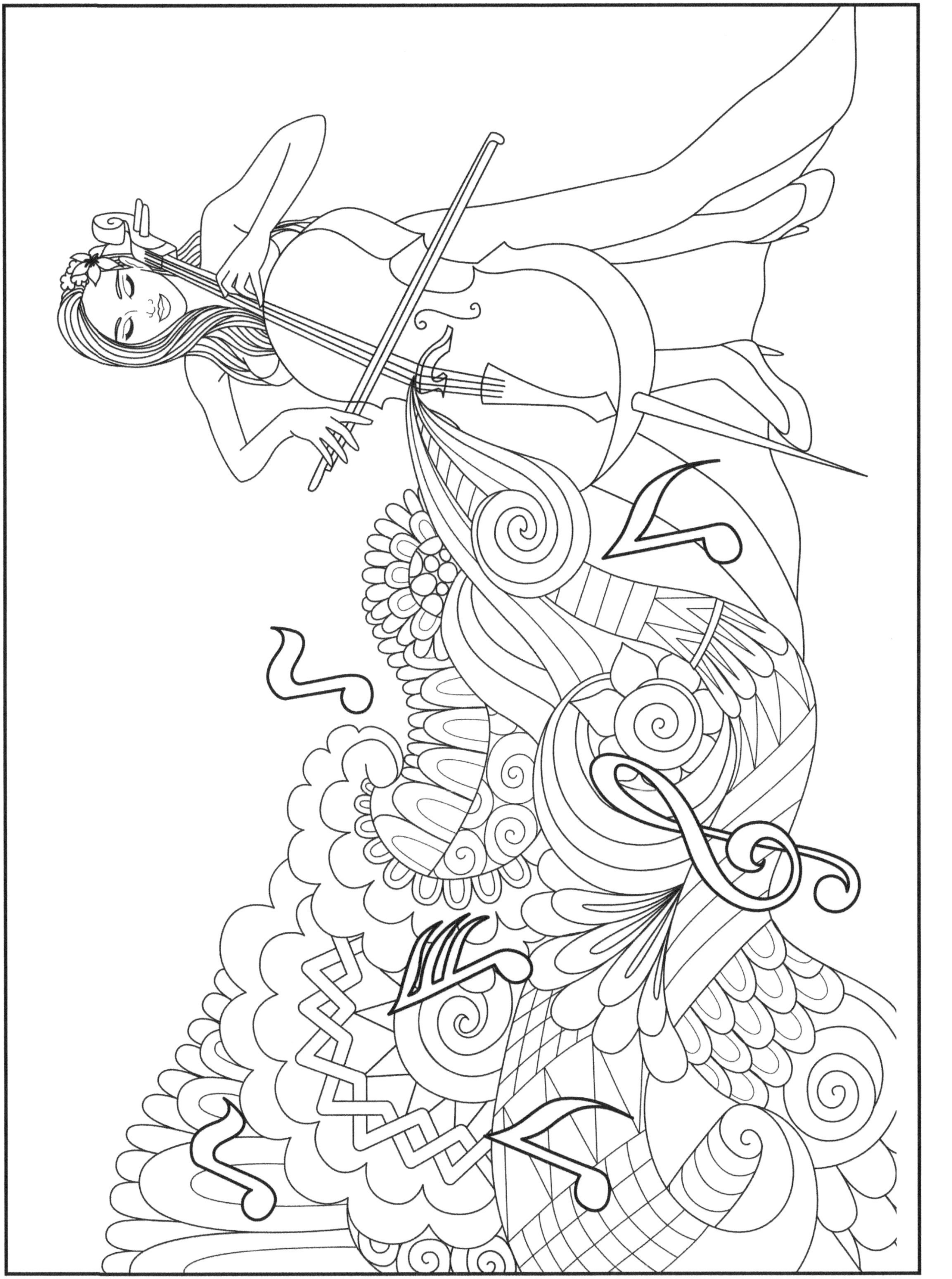

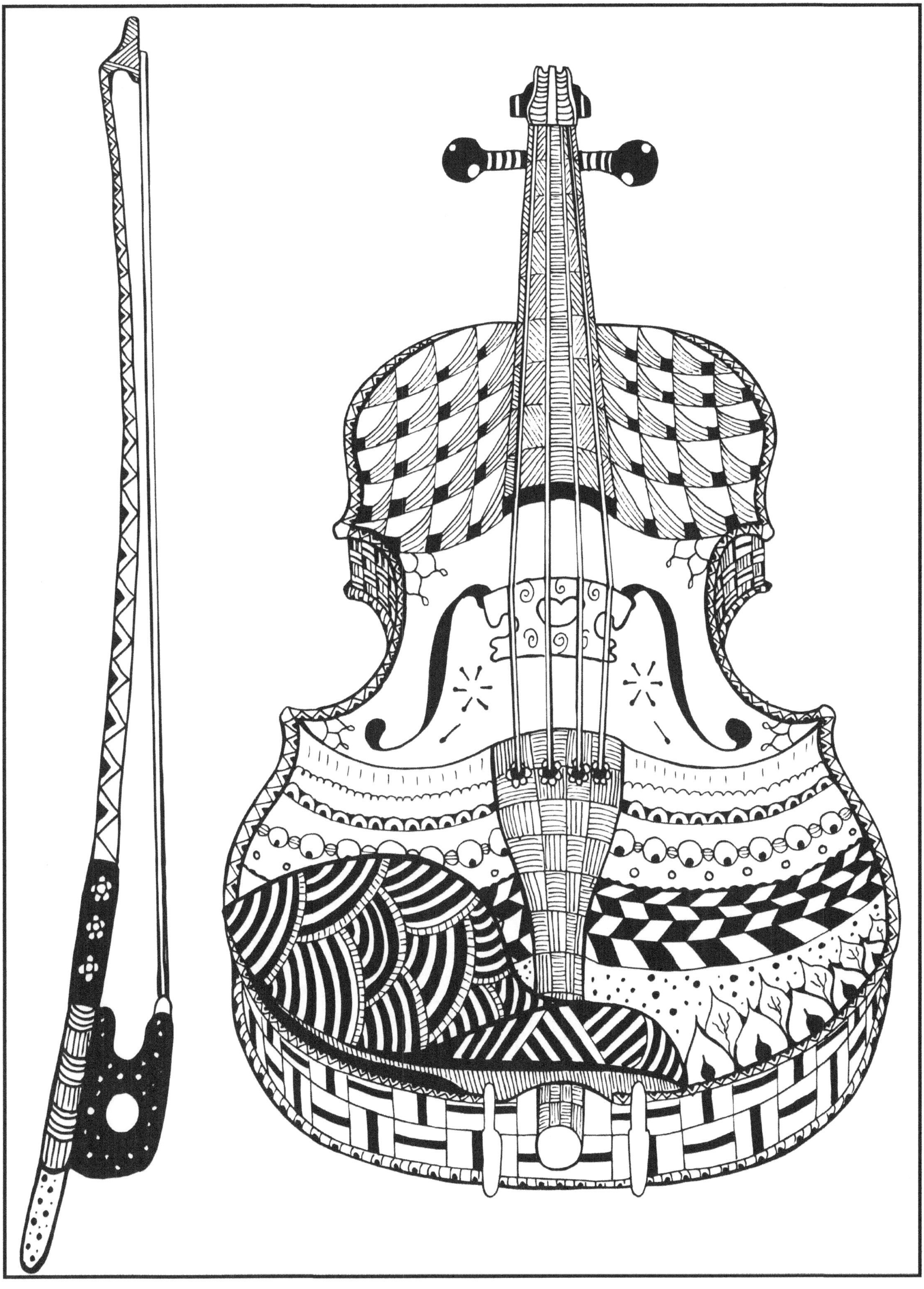

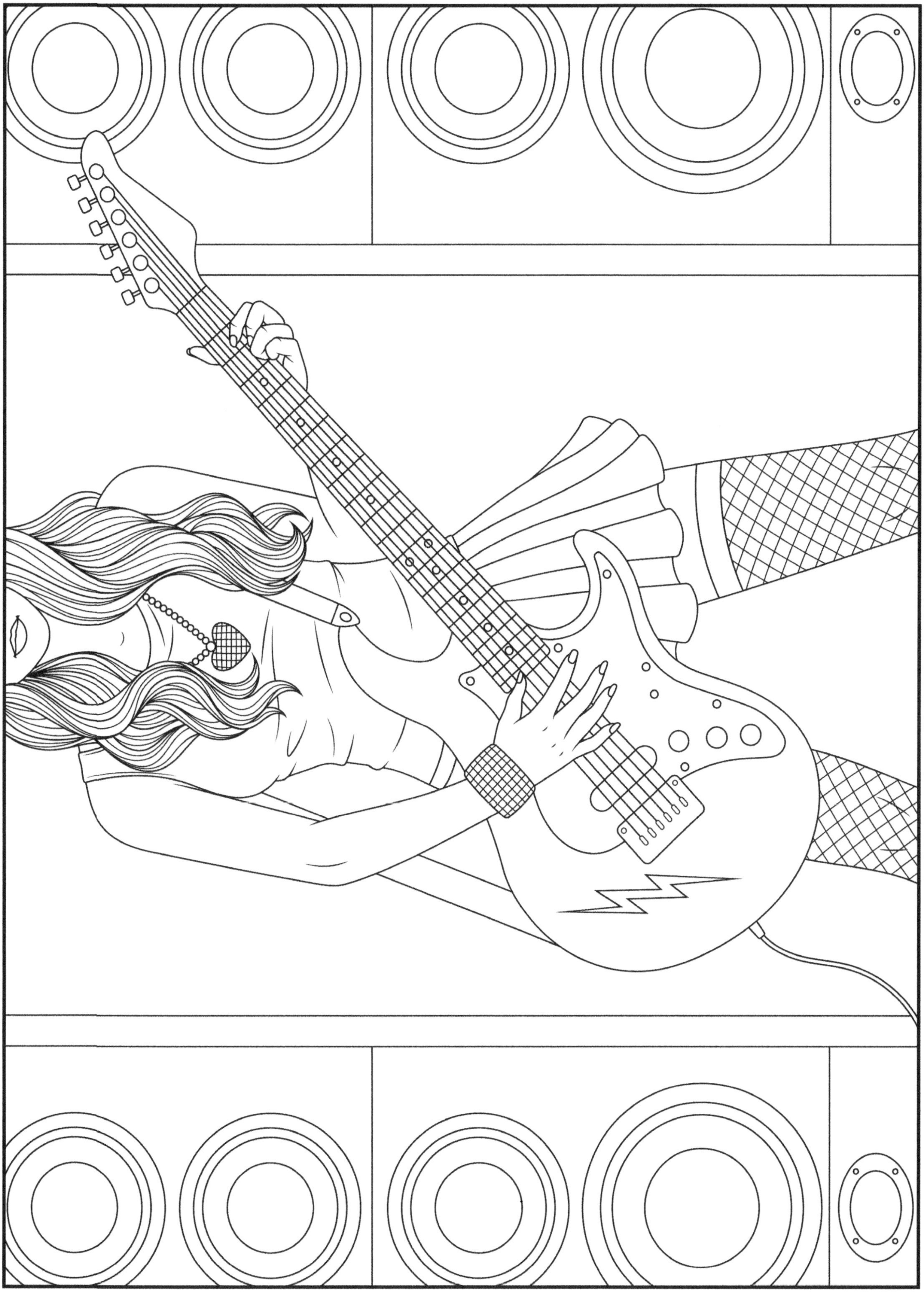

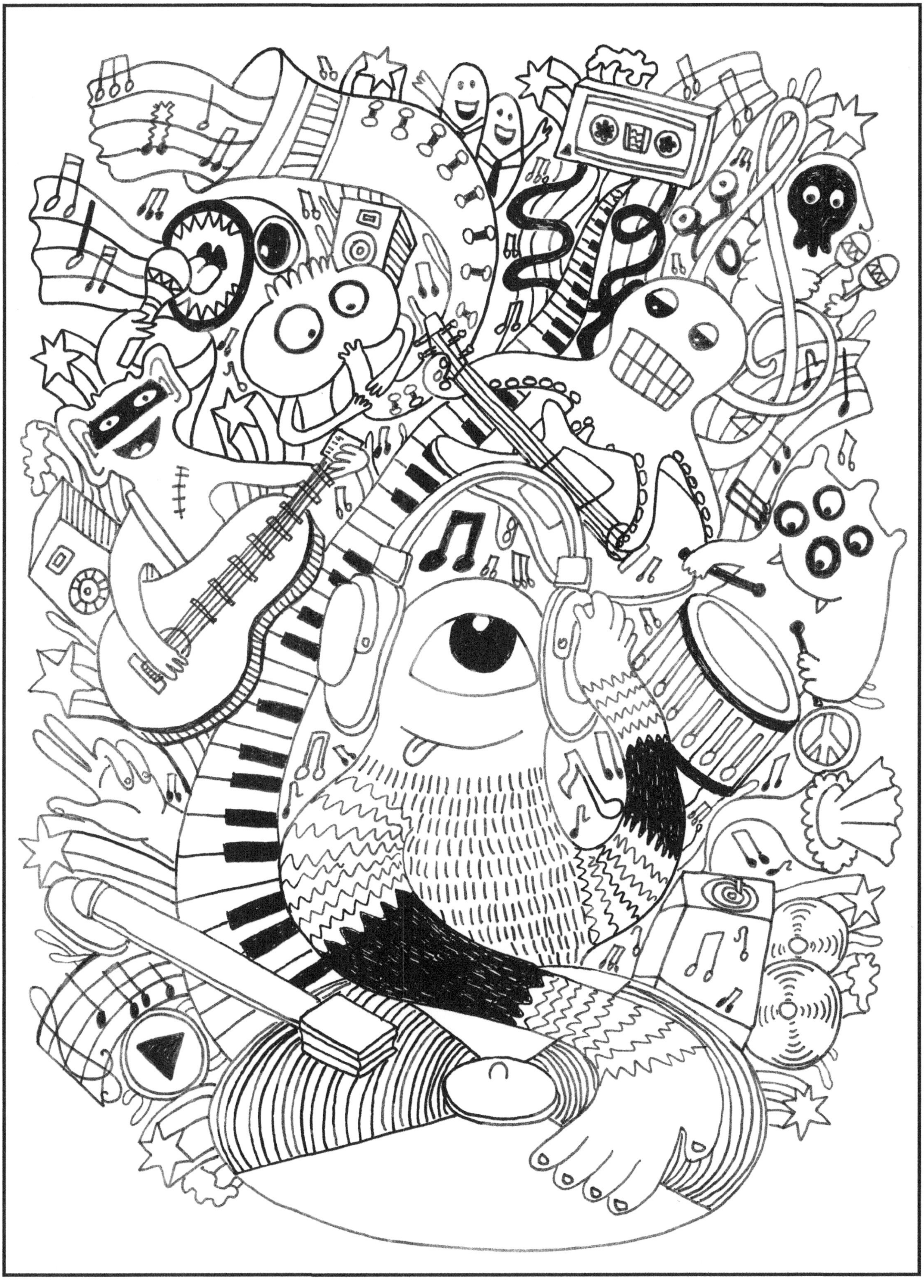

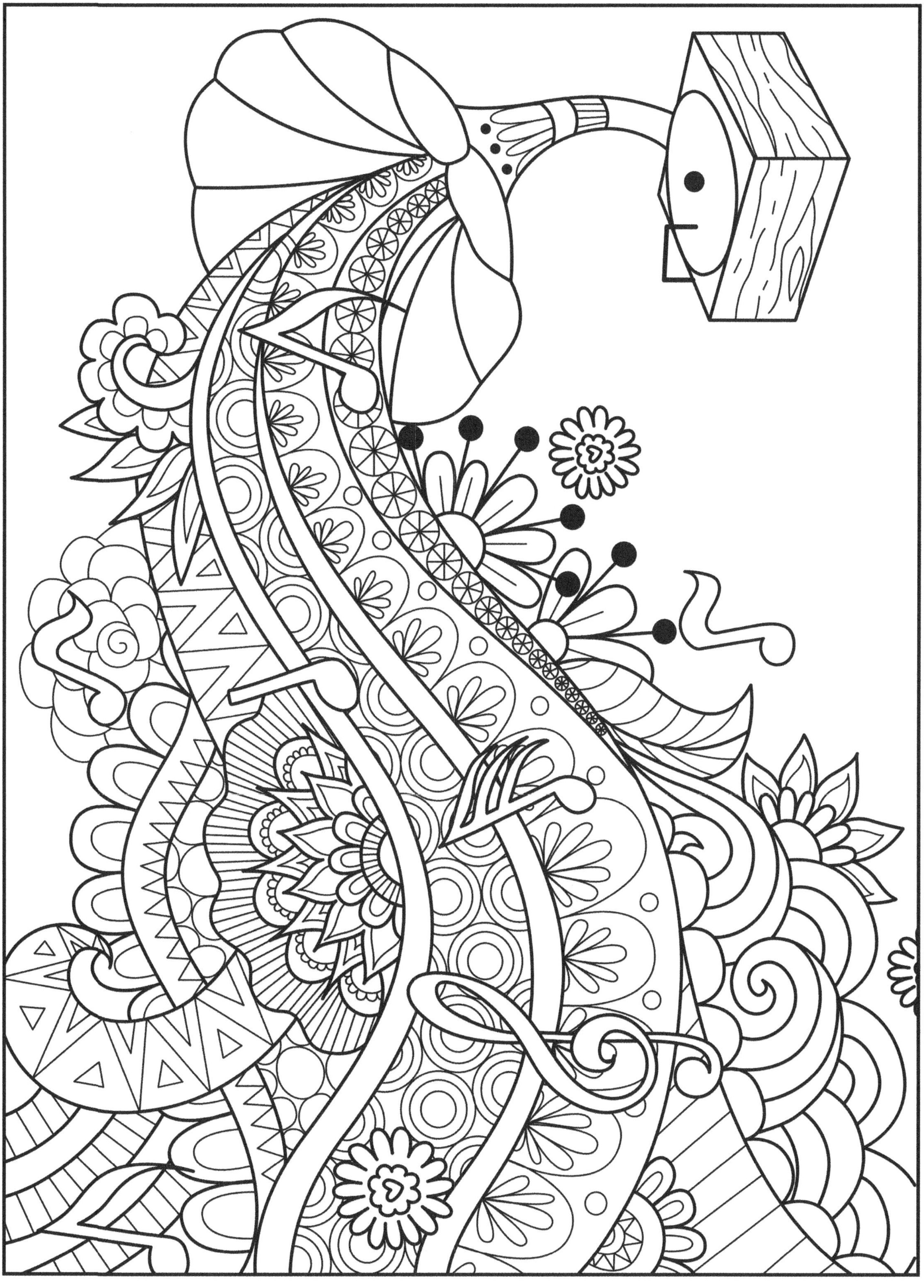

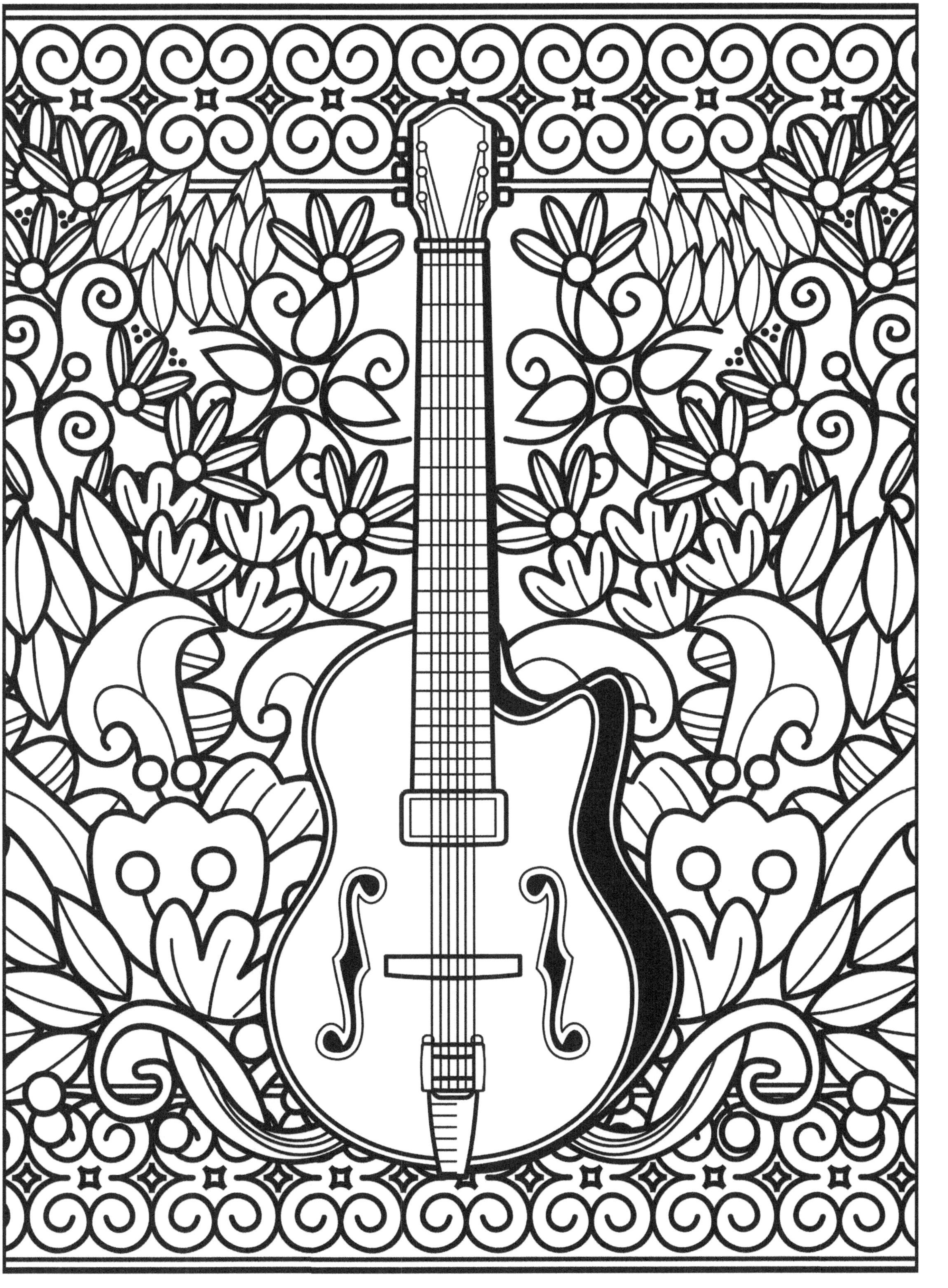

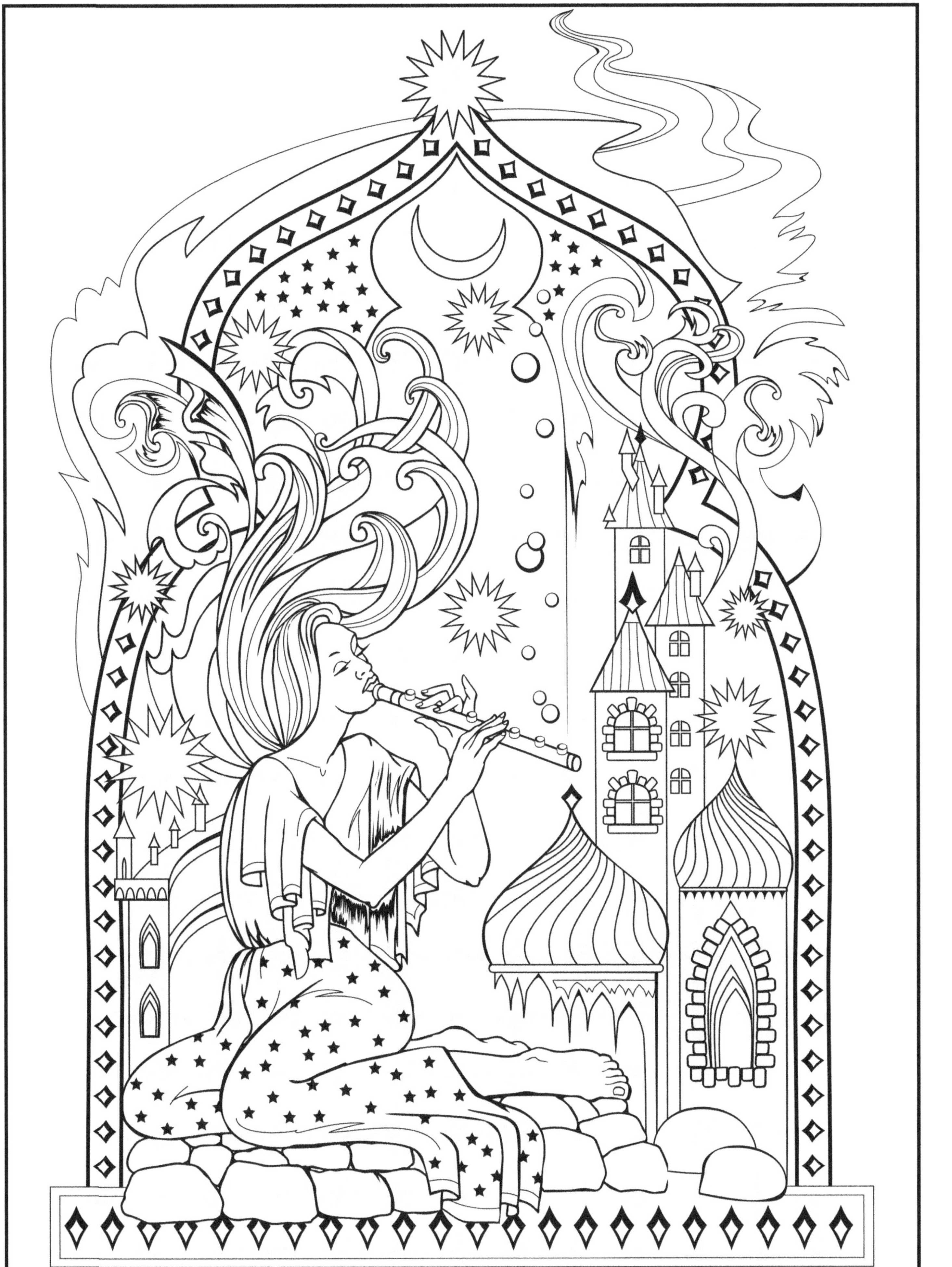

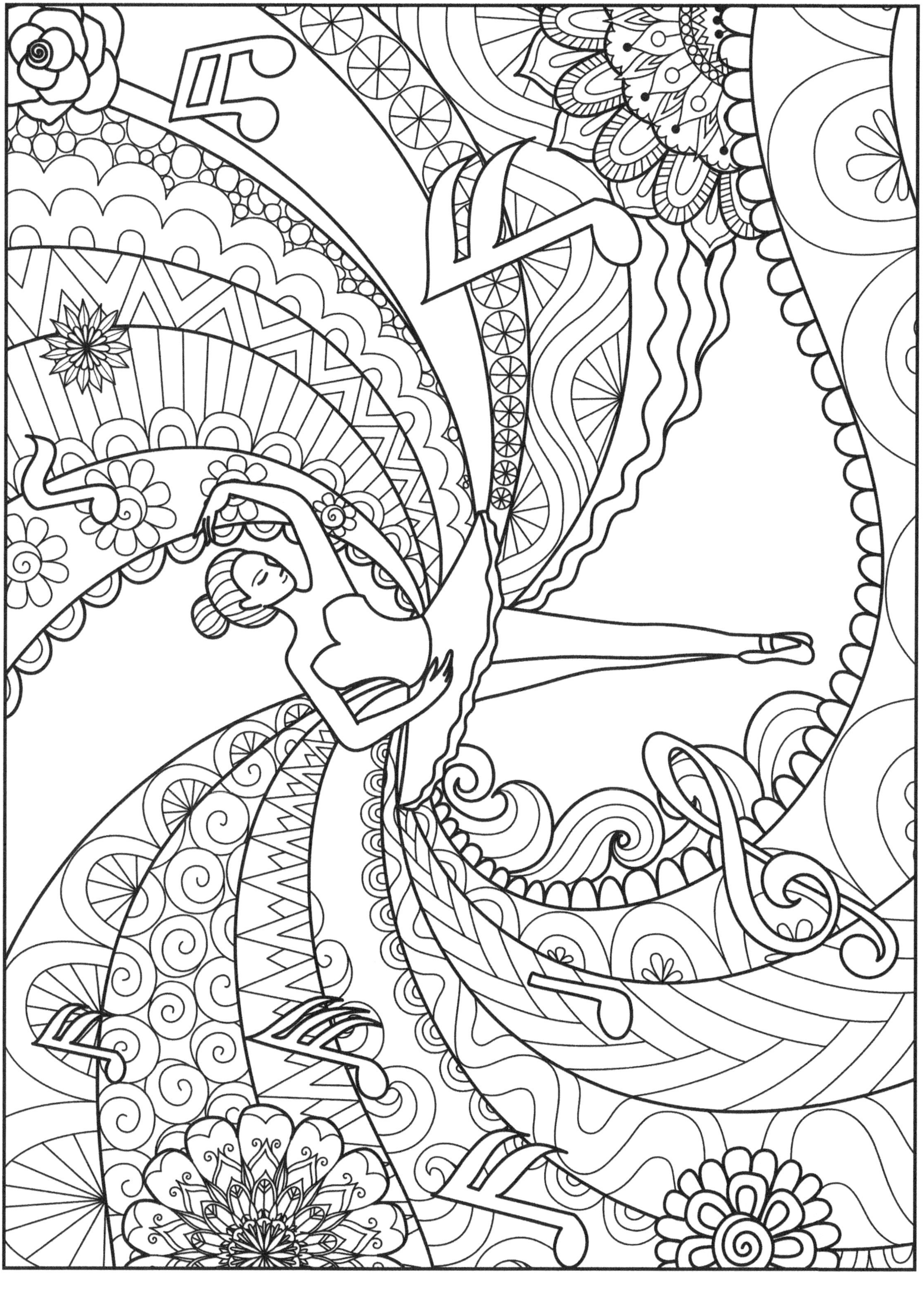

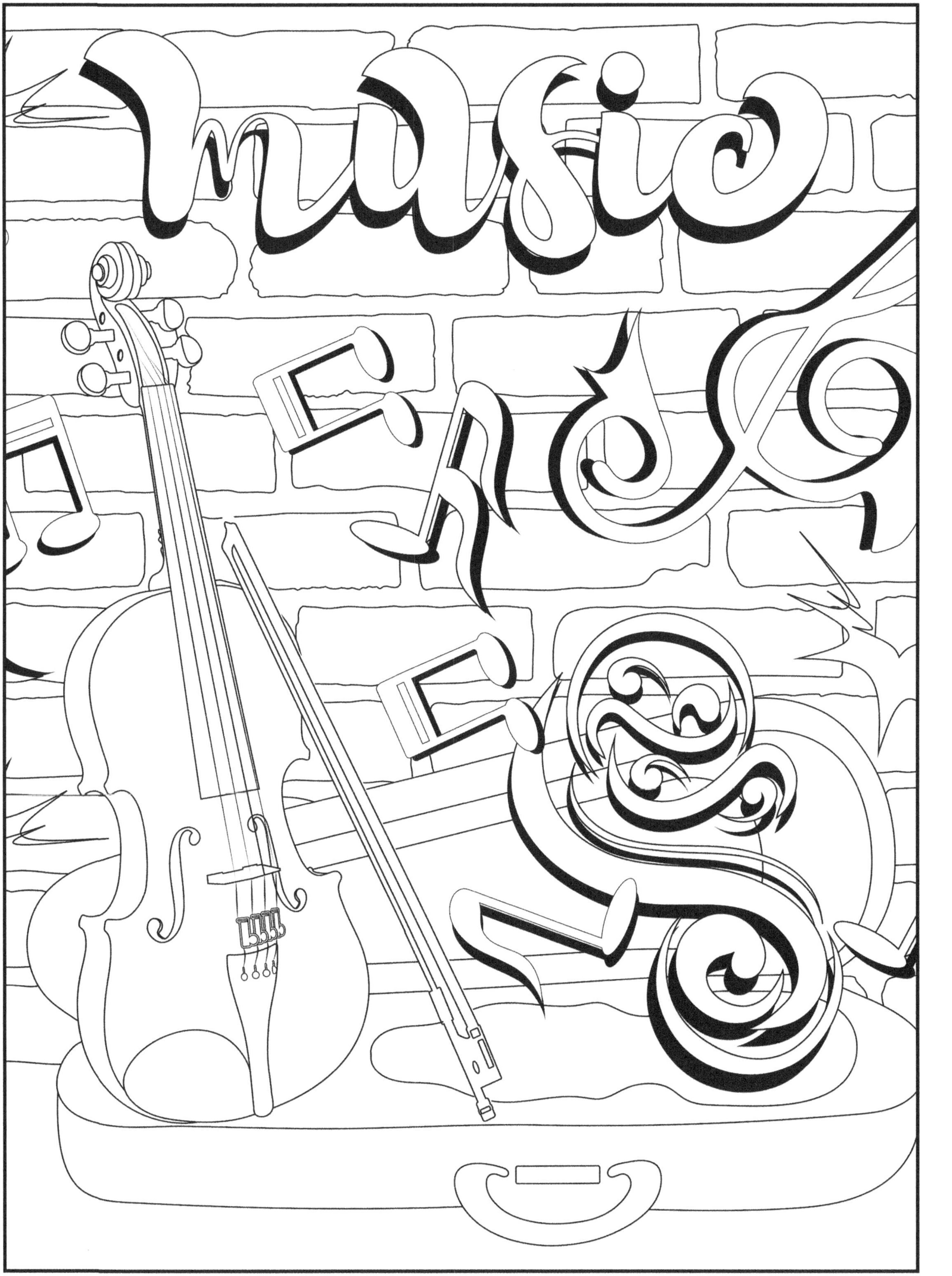
Music

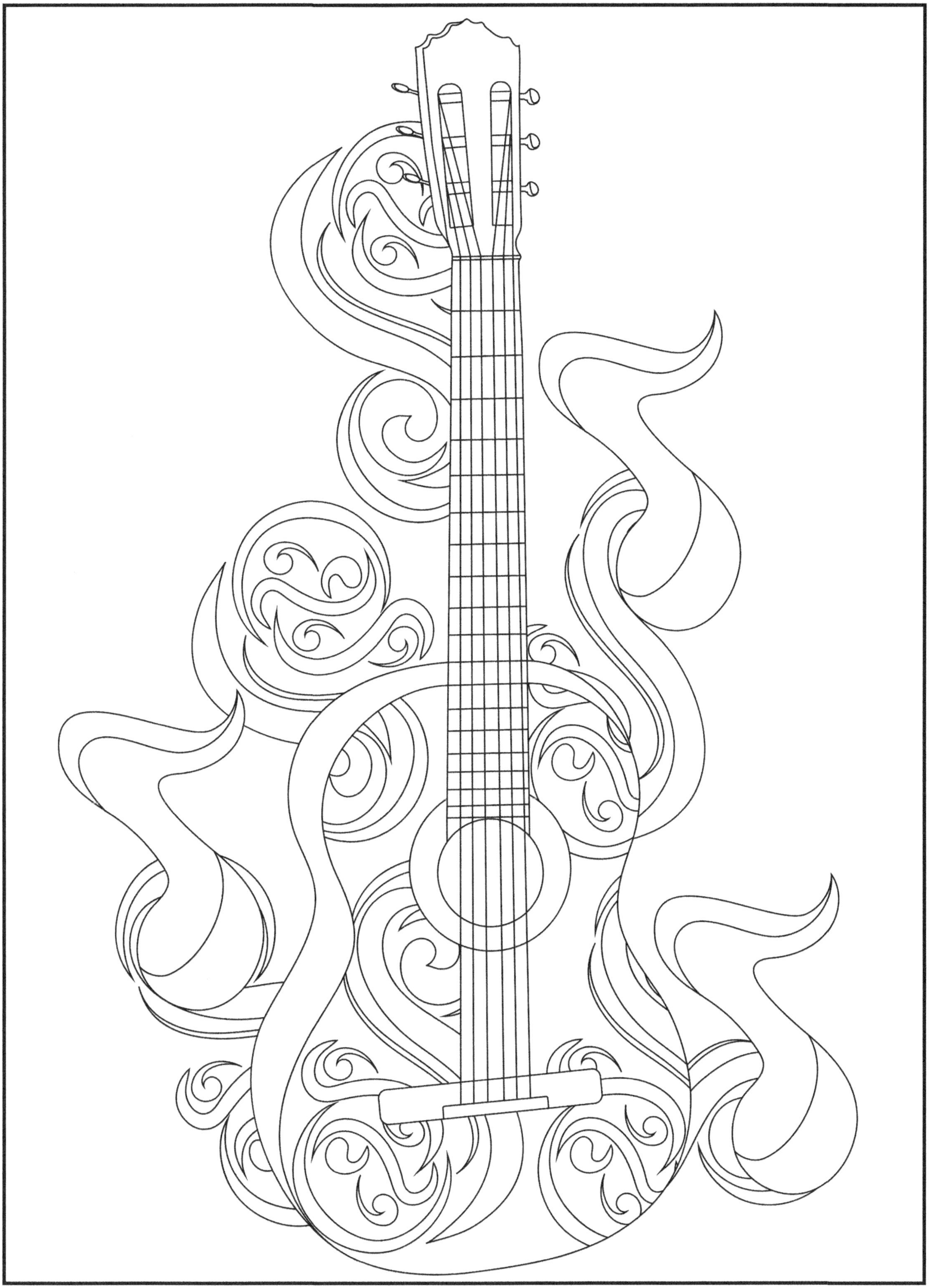

Listen to nature

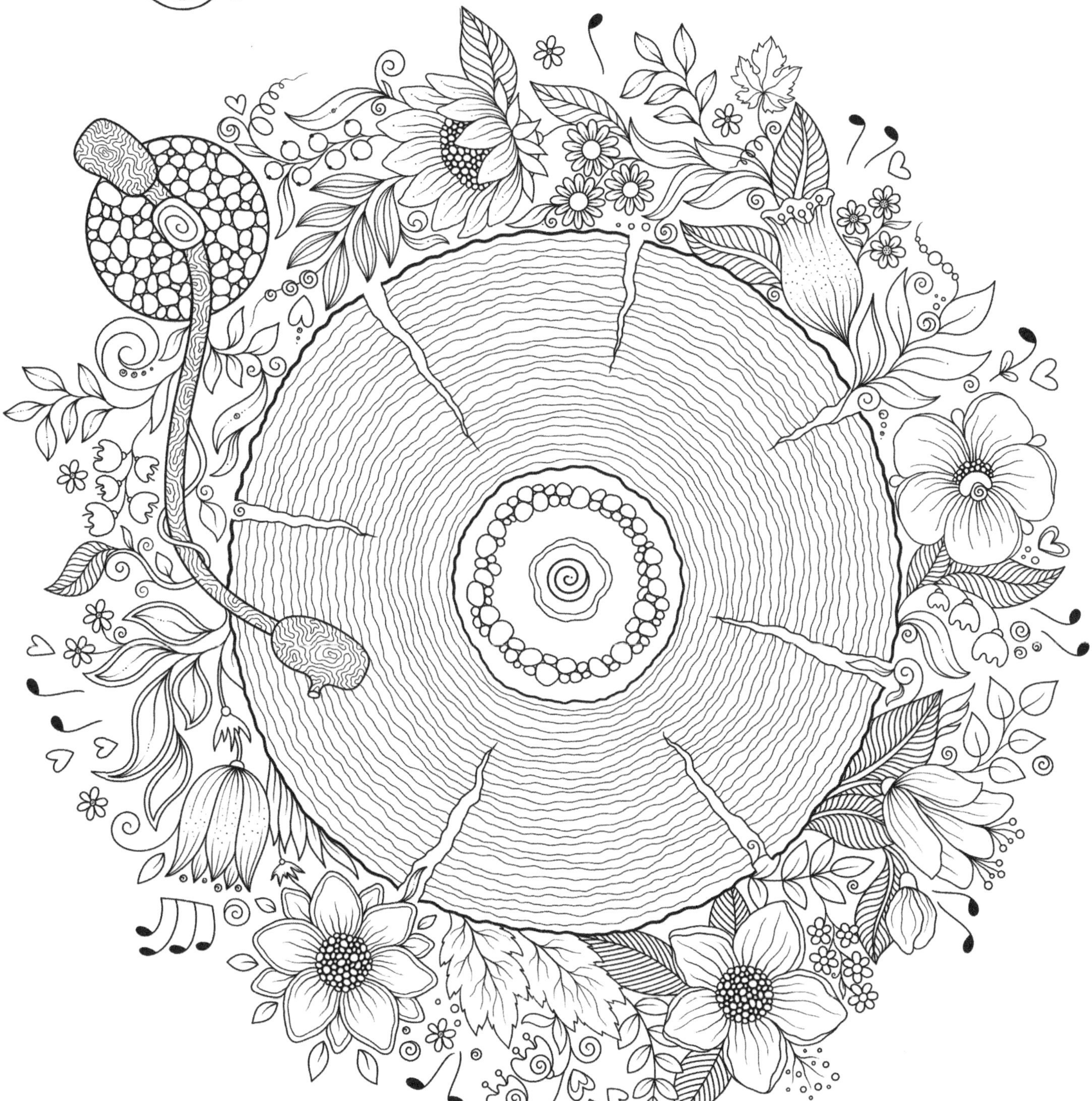

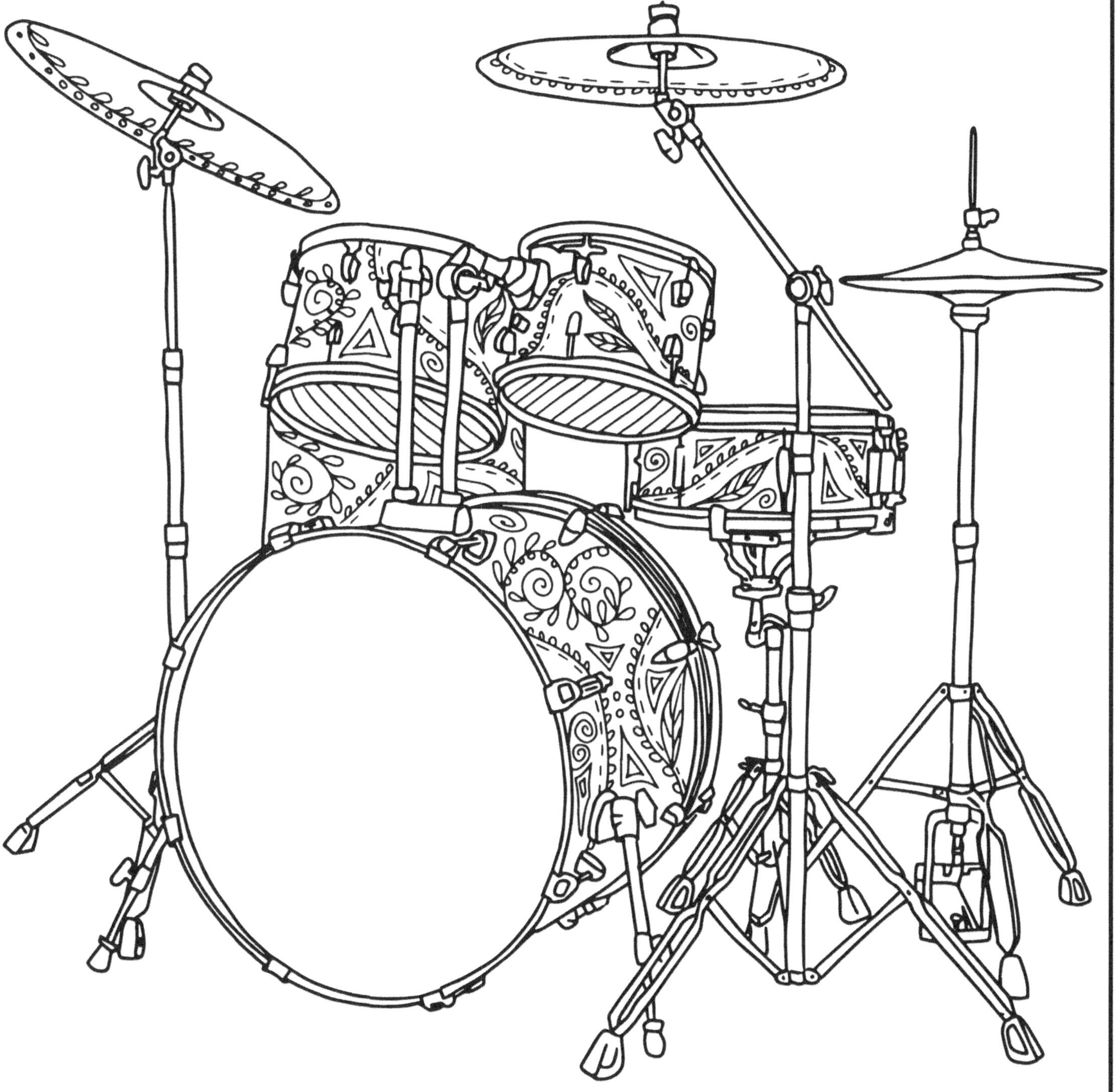

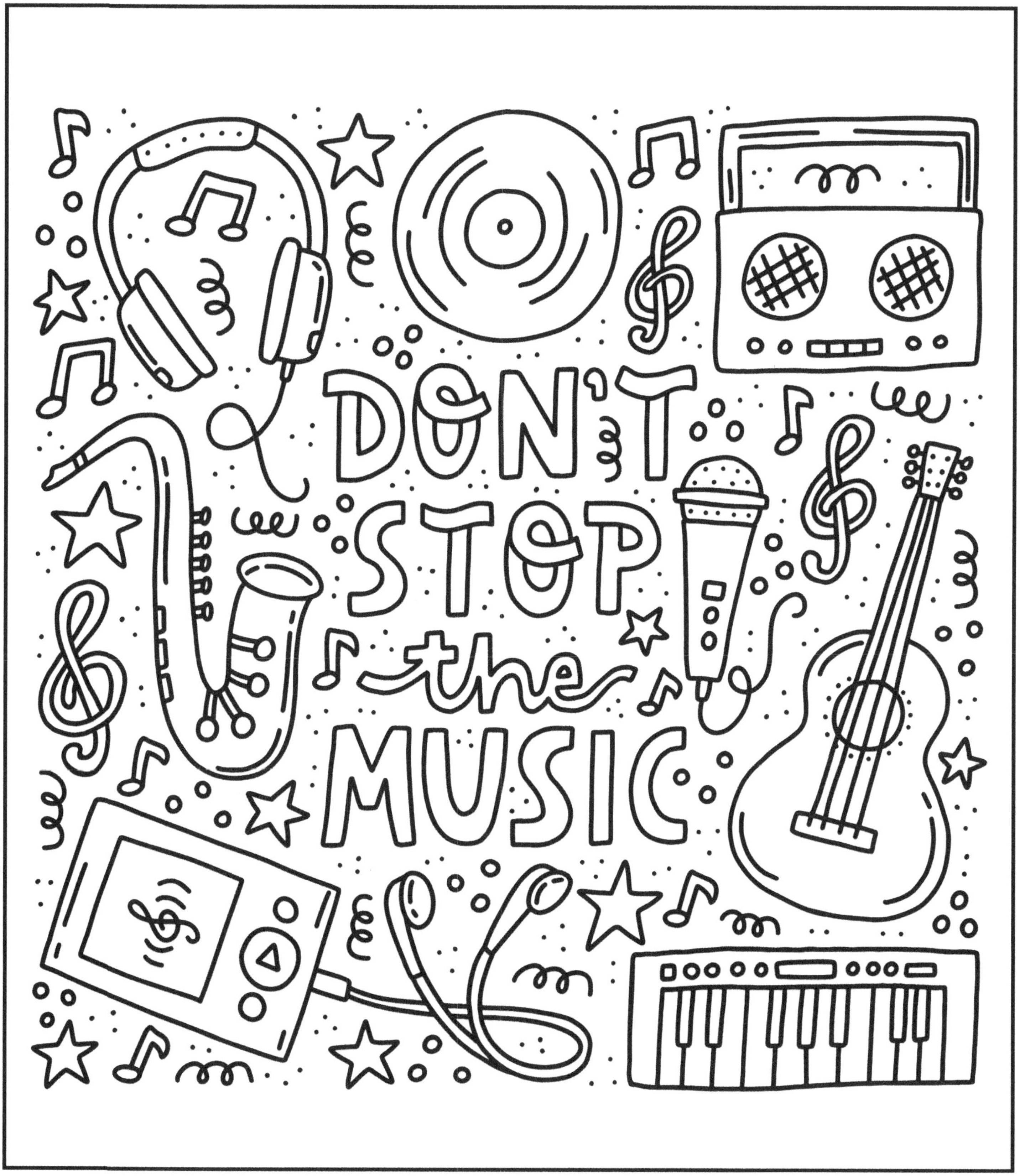
DON'T STOP the MUSIC

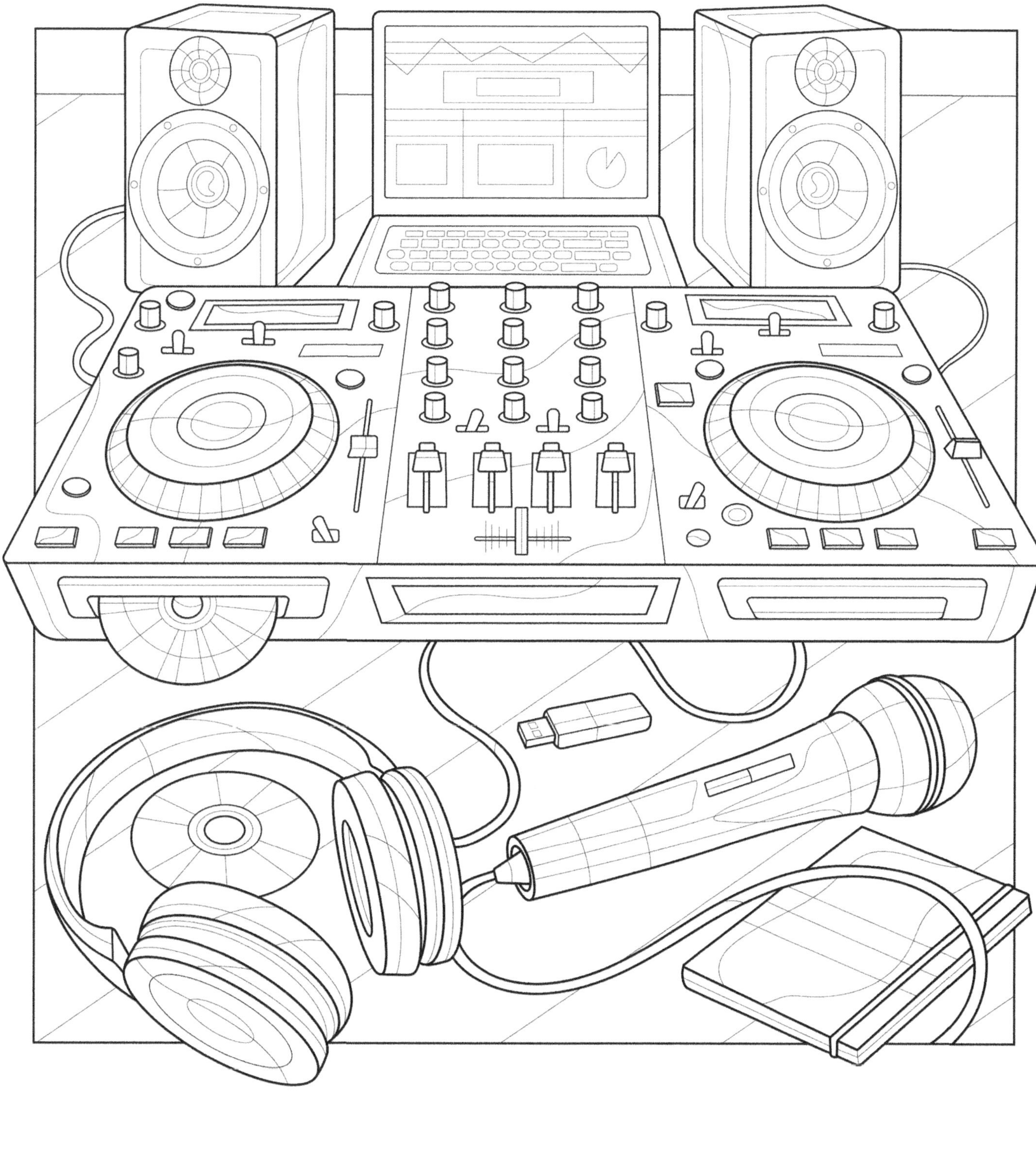

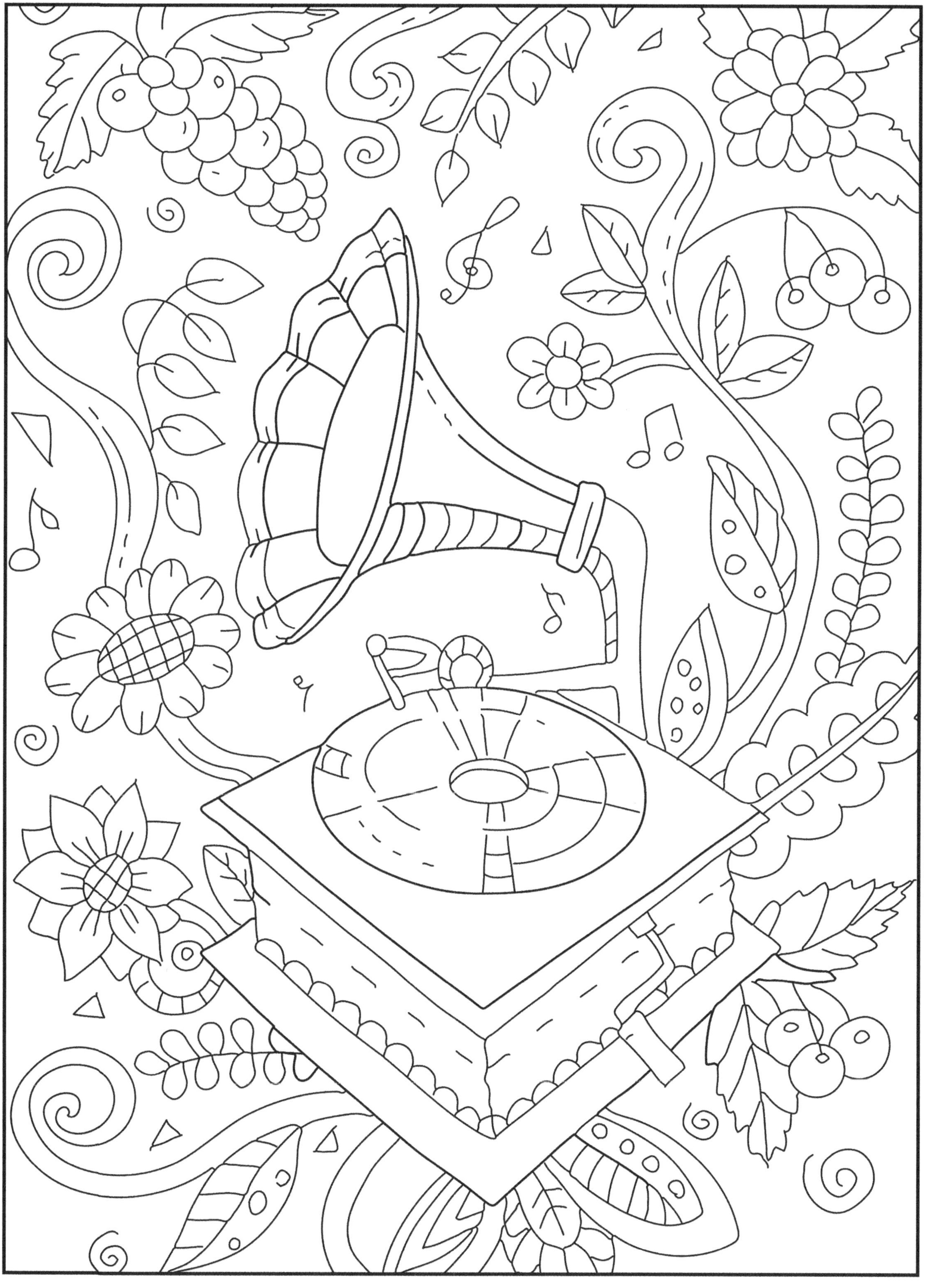

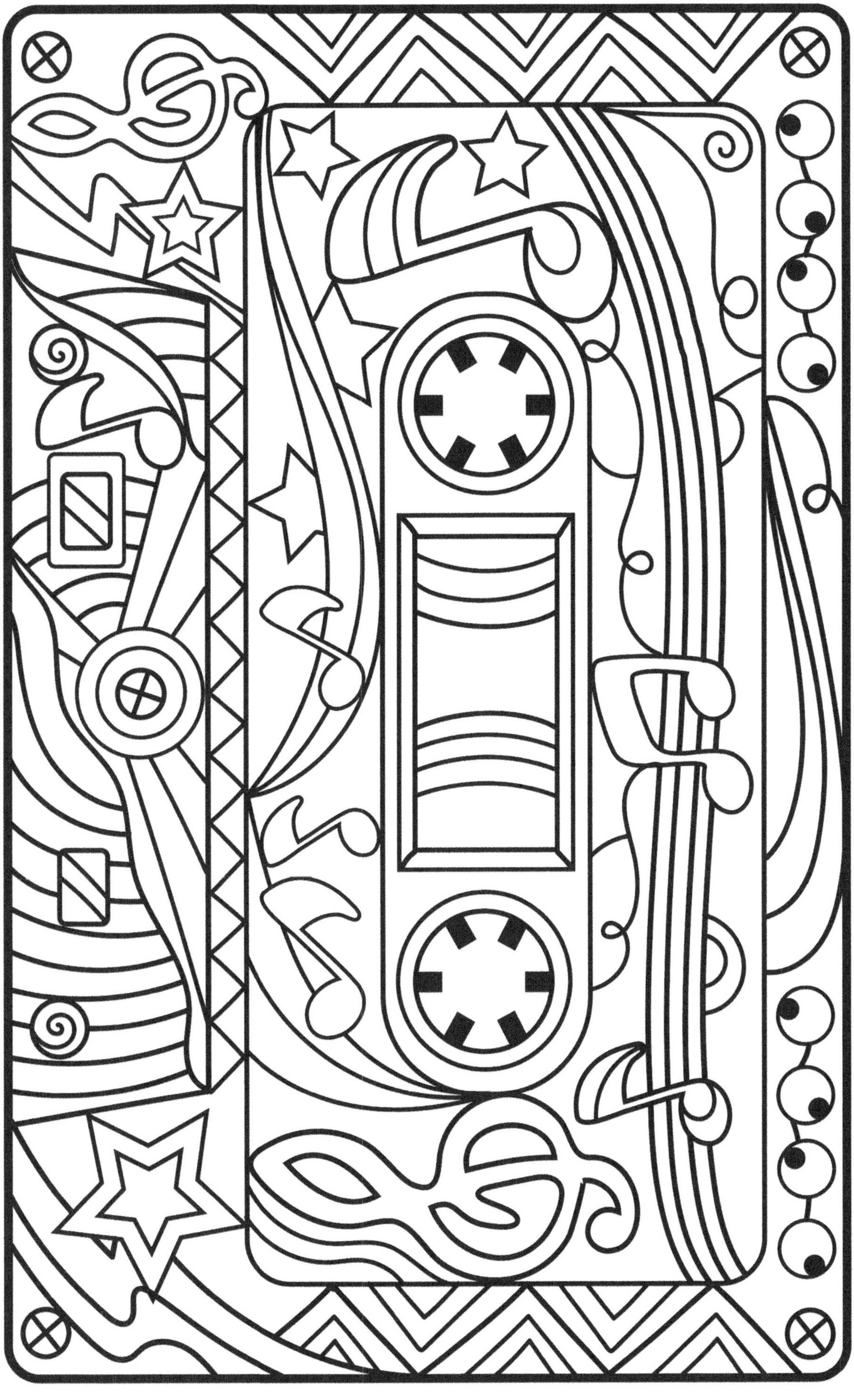

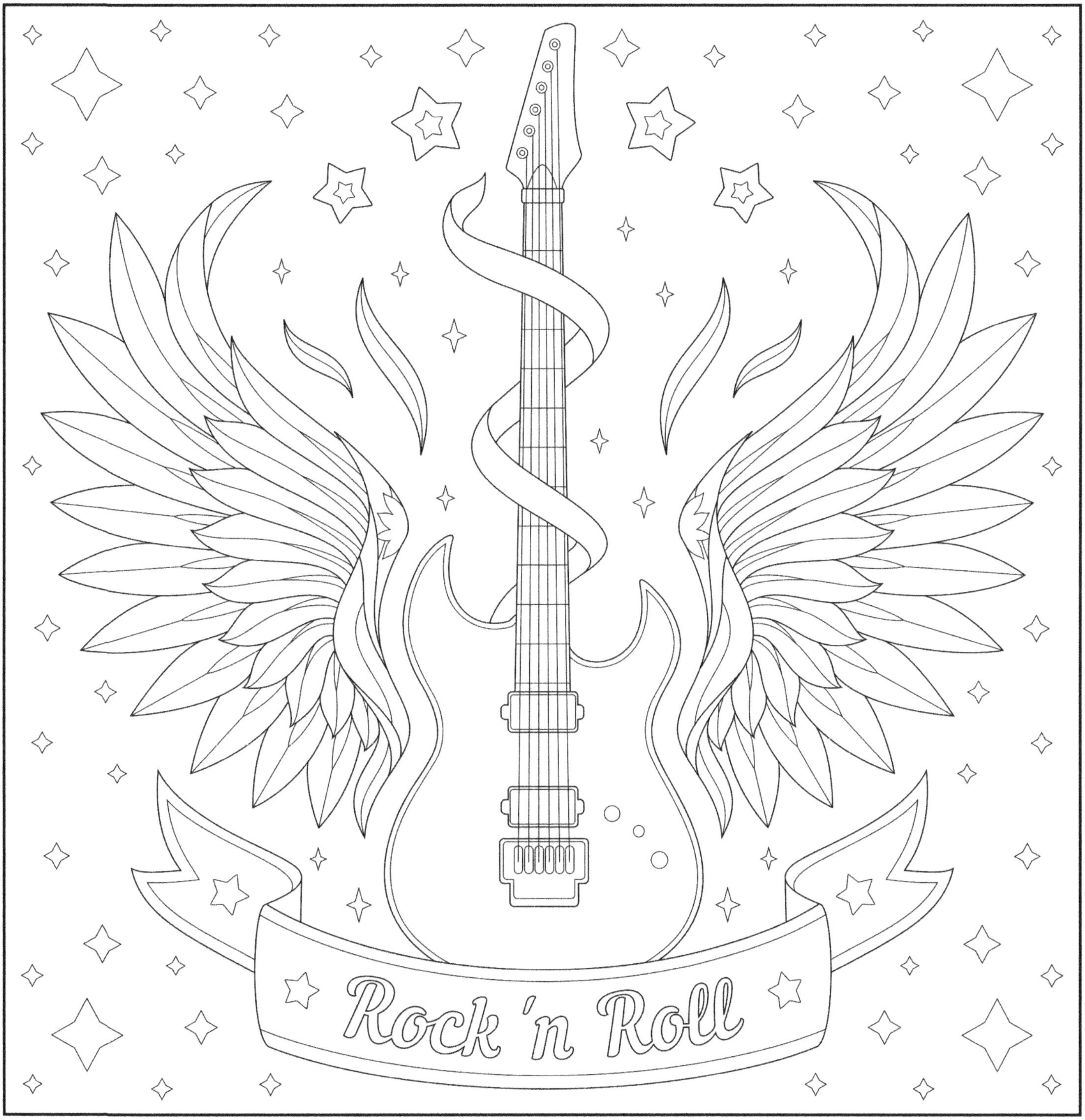
Rock 'n Roll

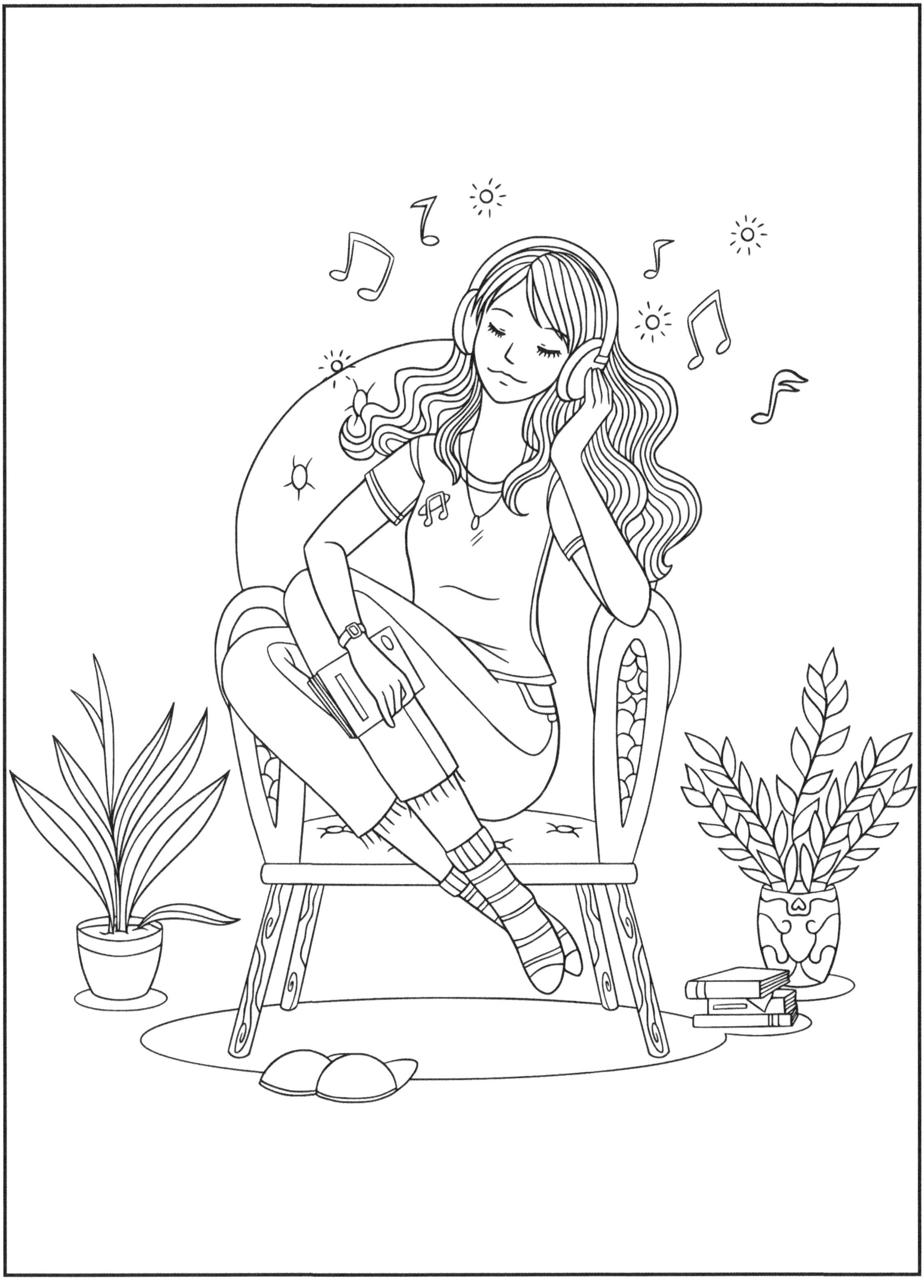

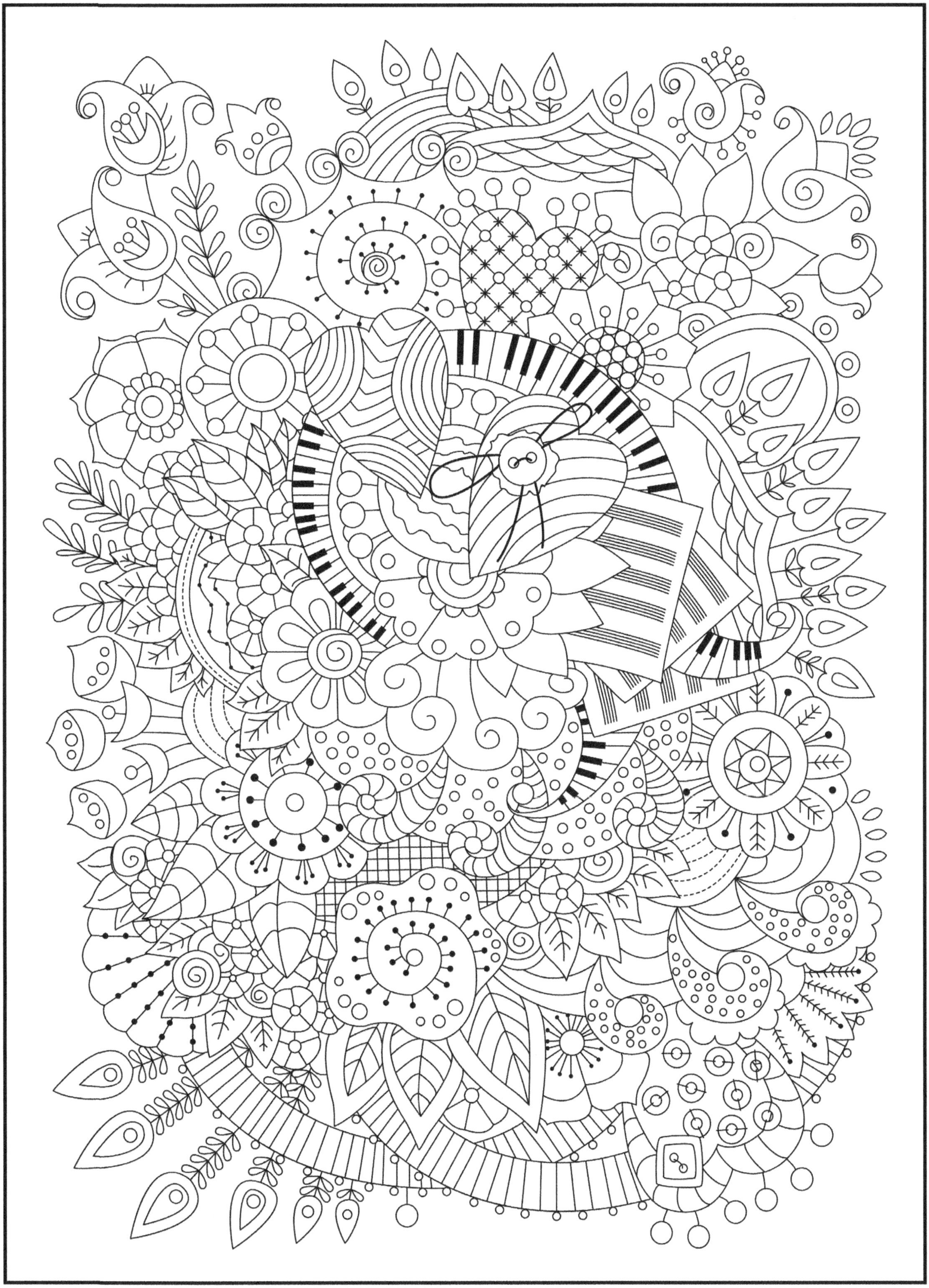

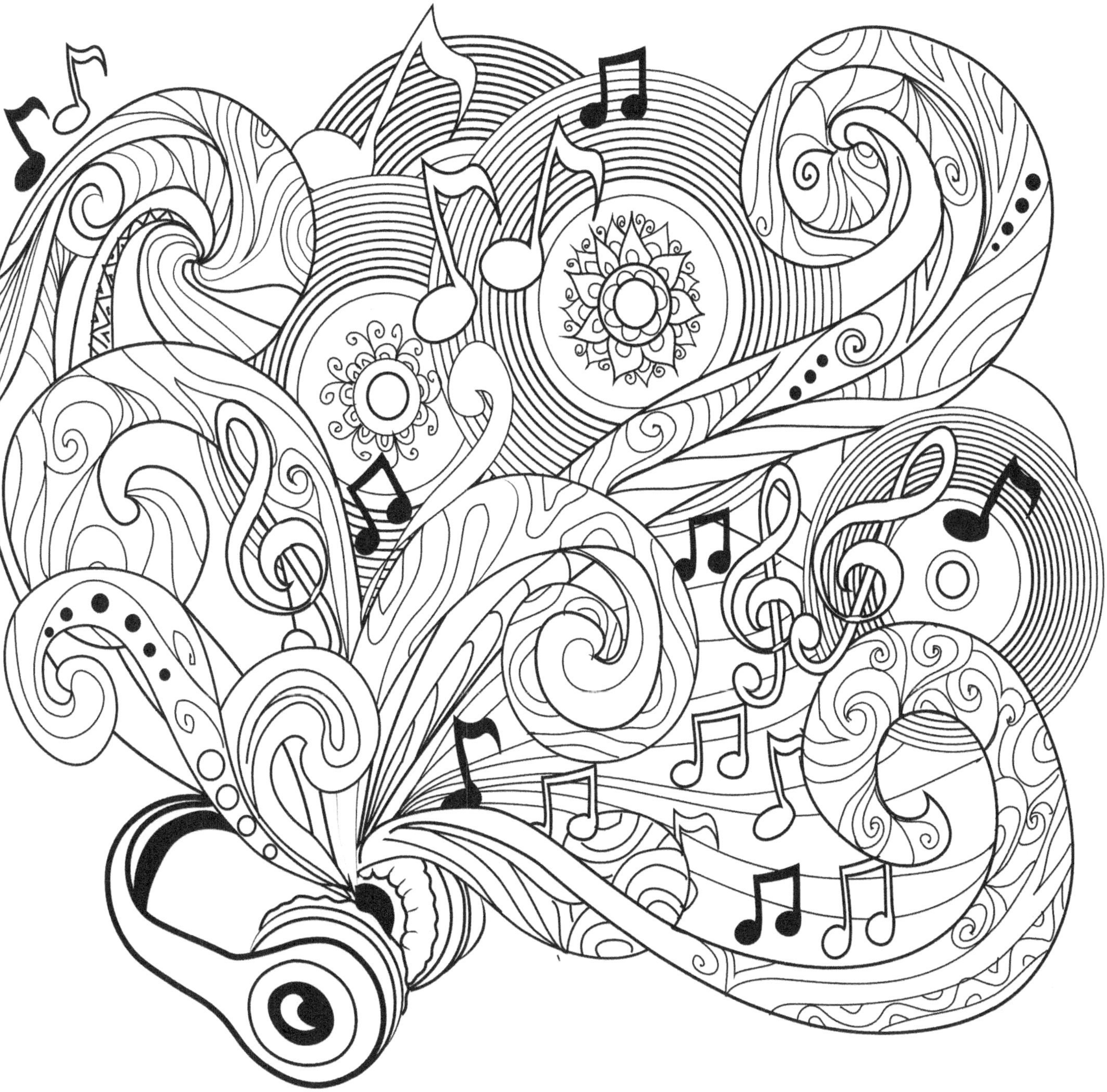

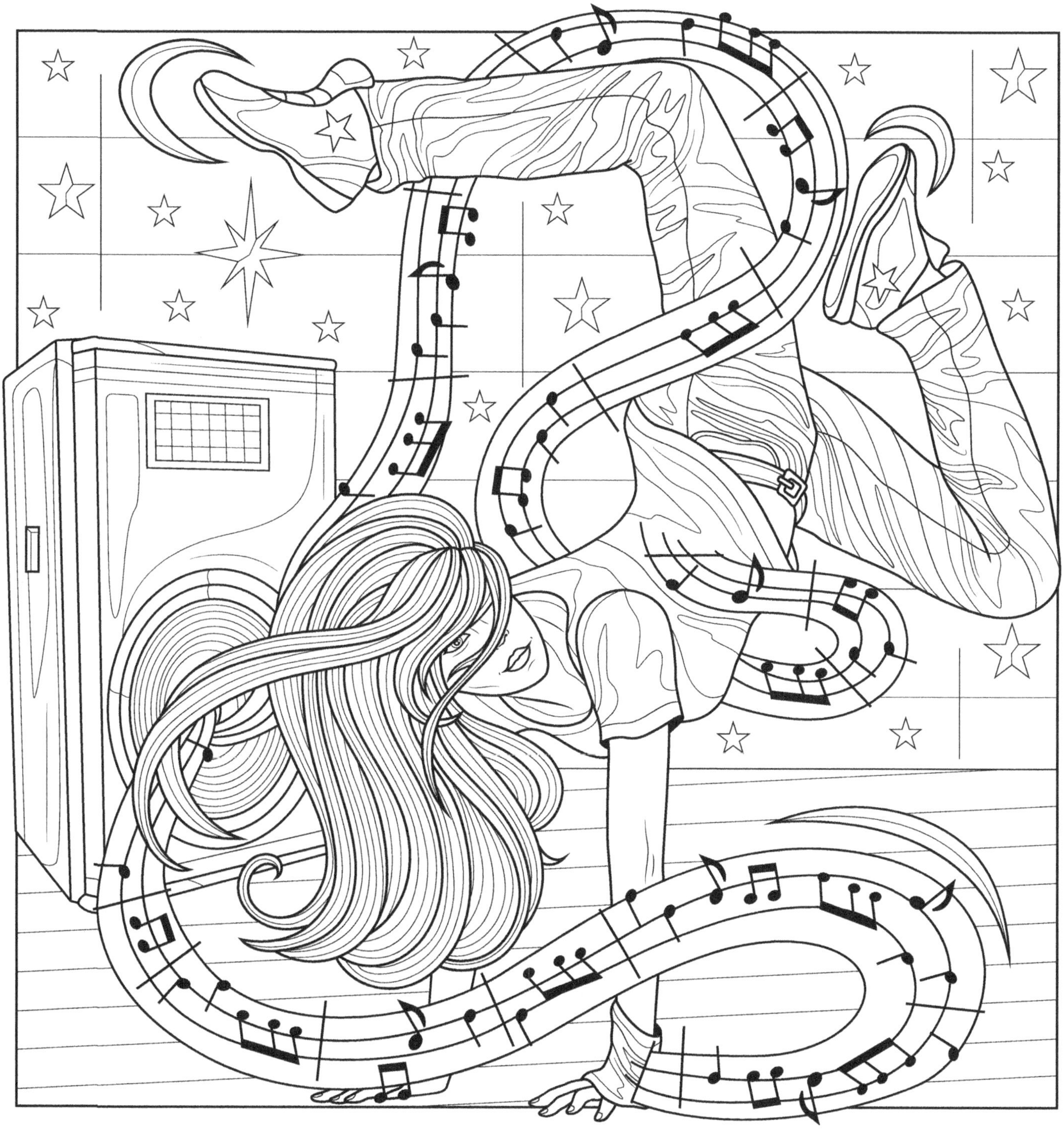

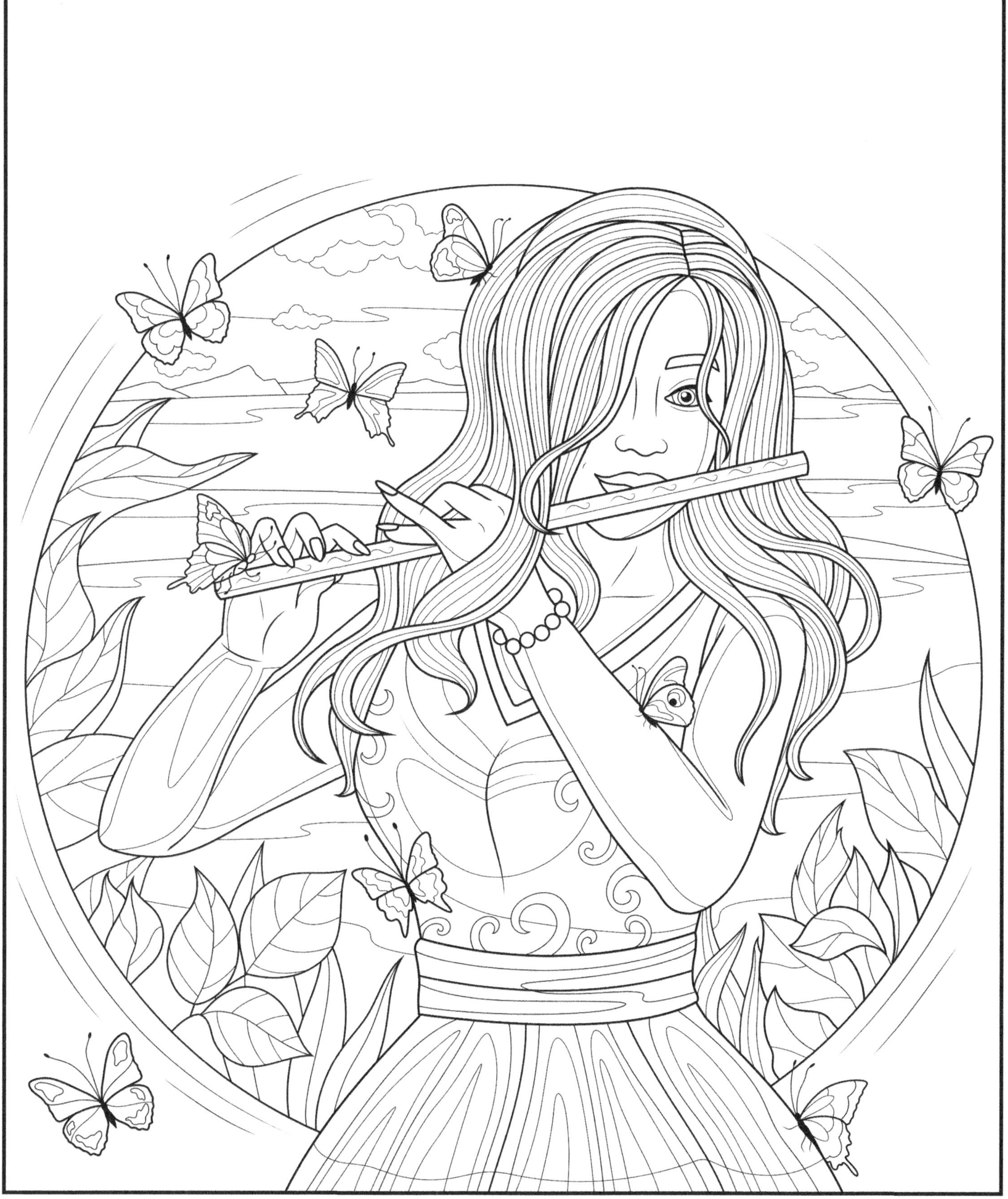

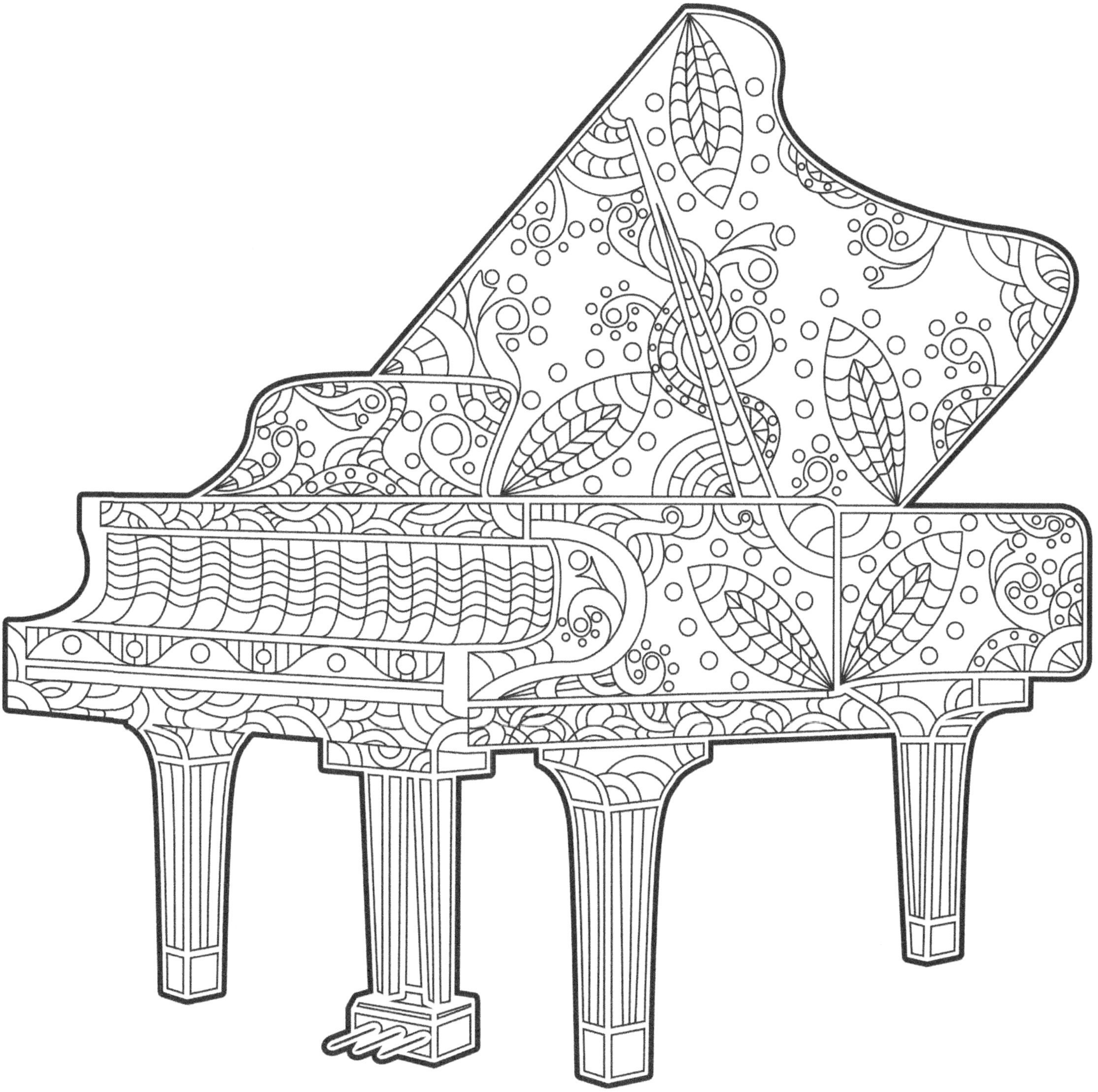

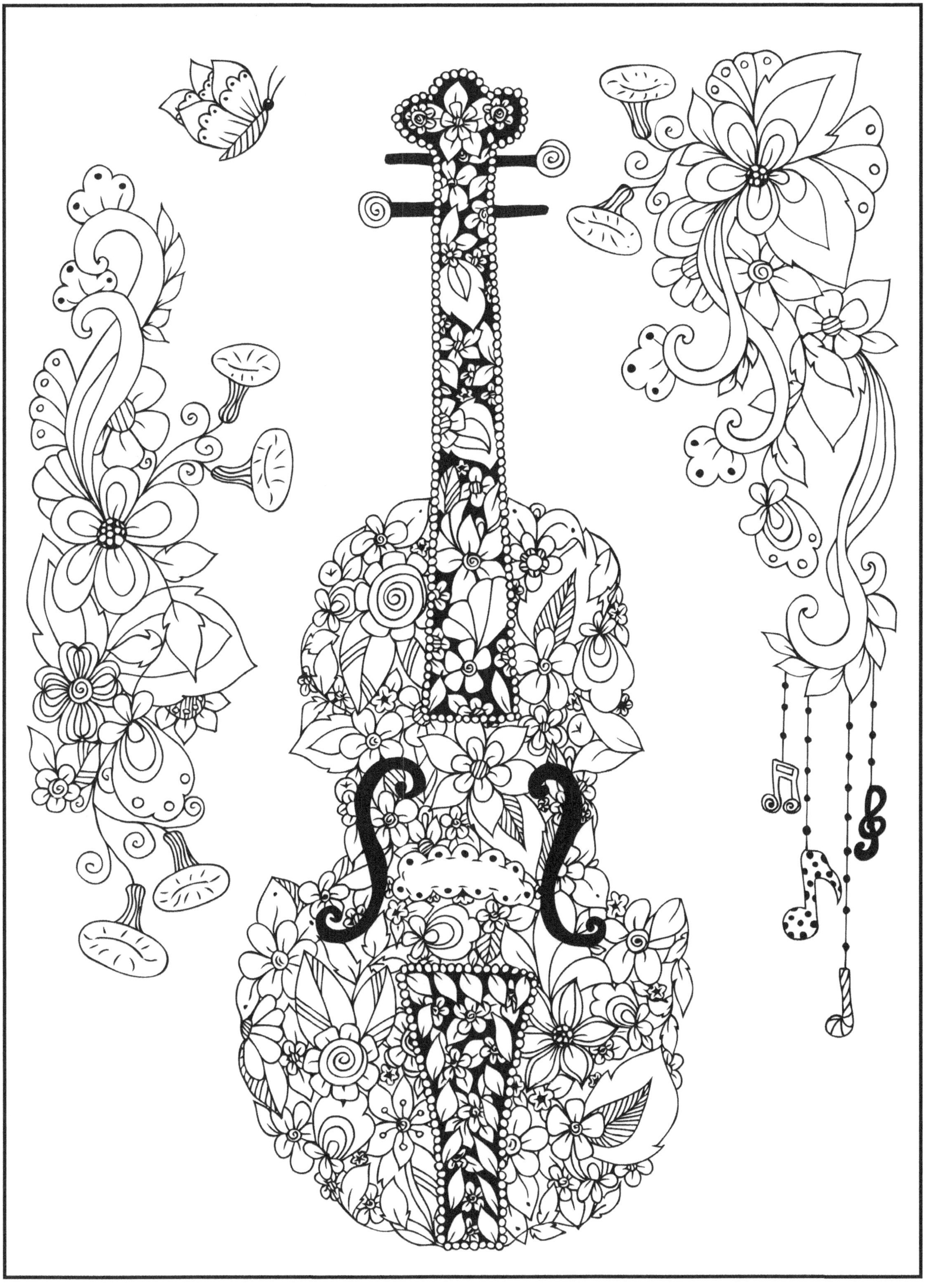

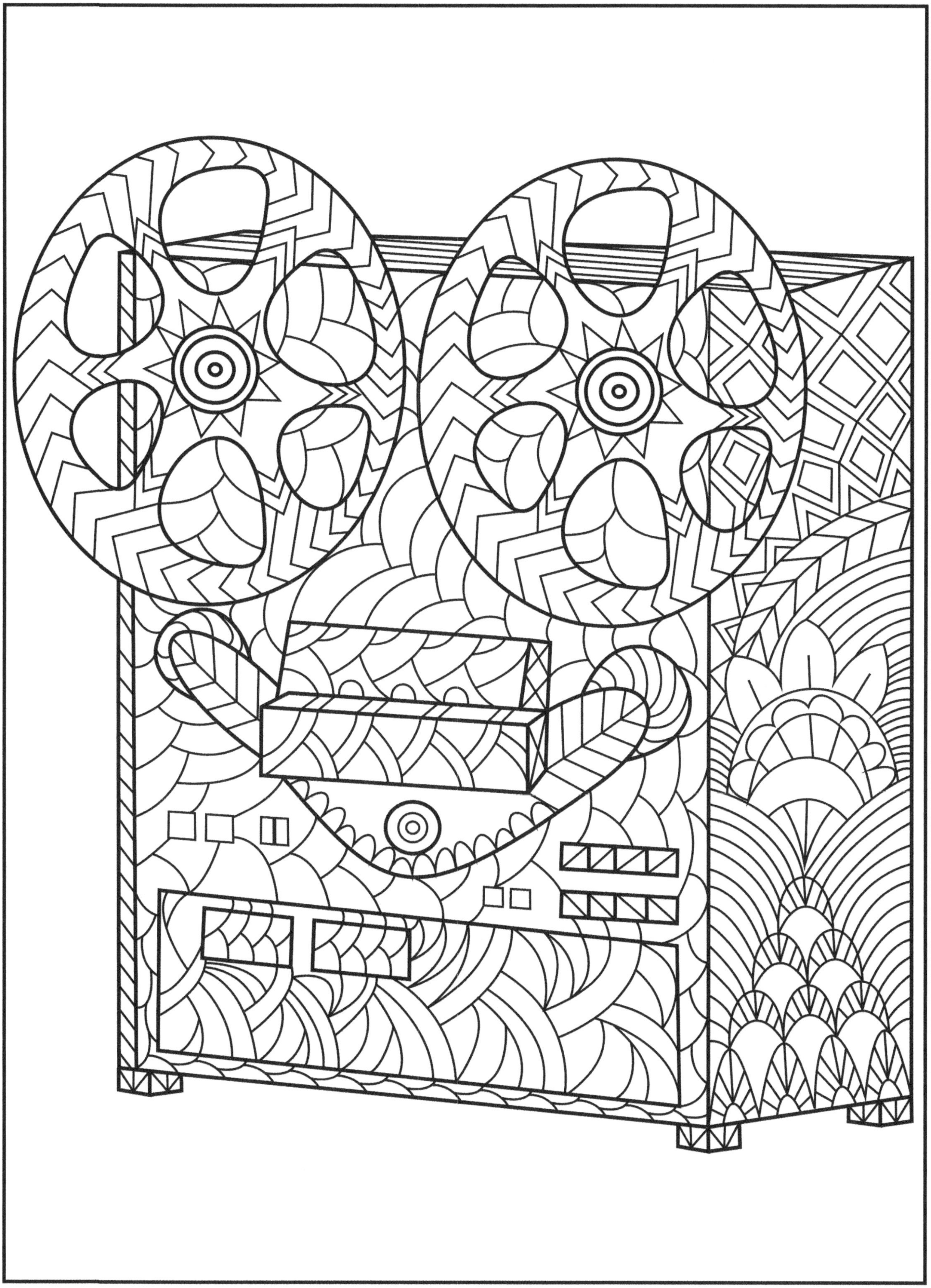

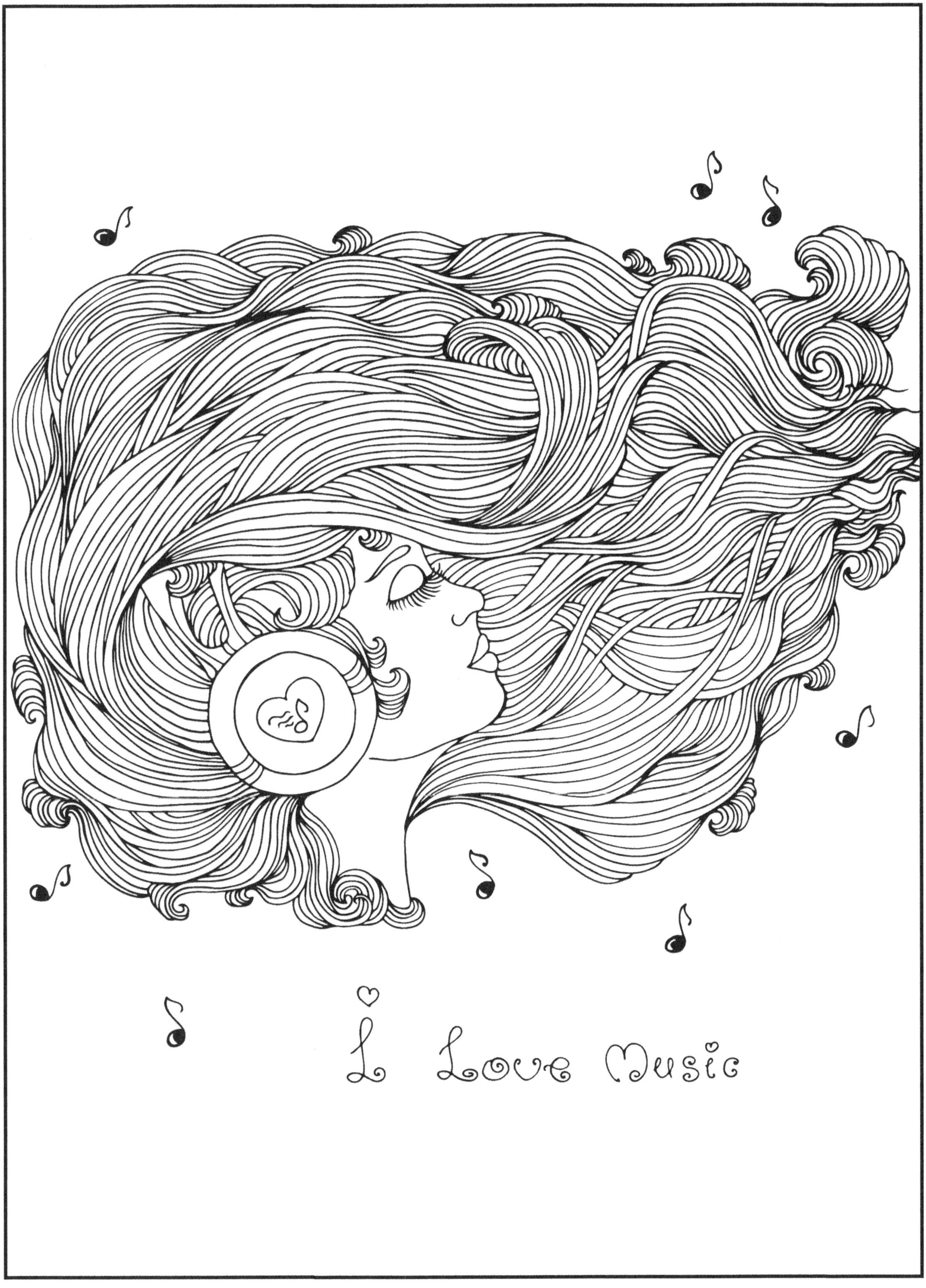
I Love Music

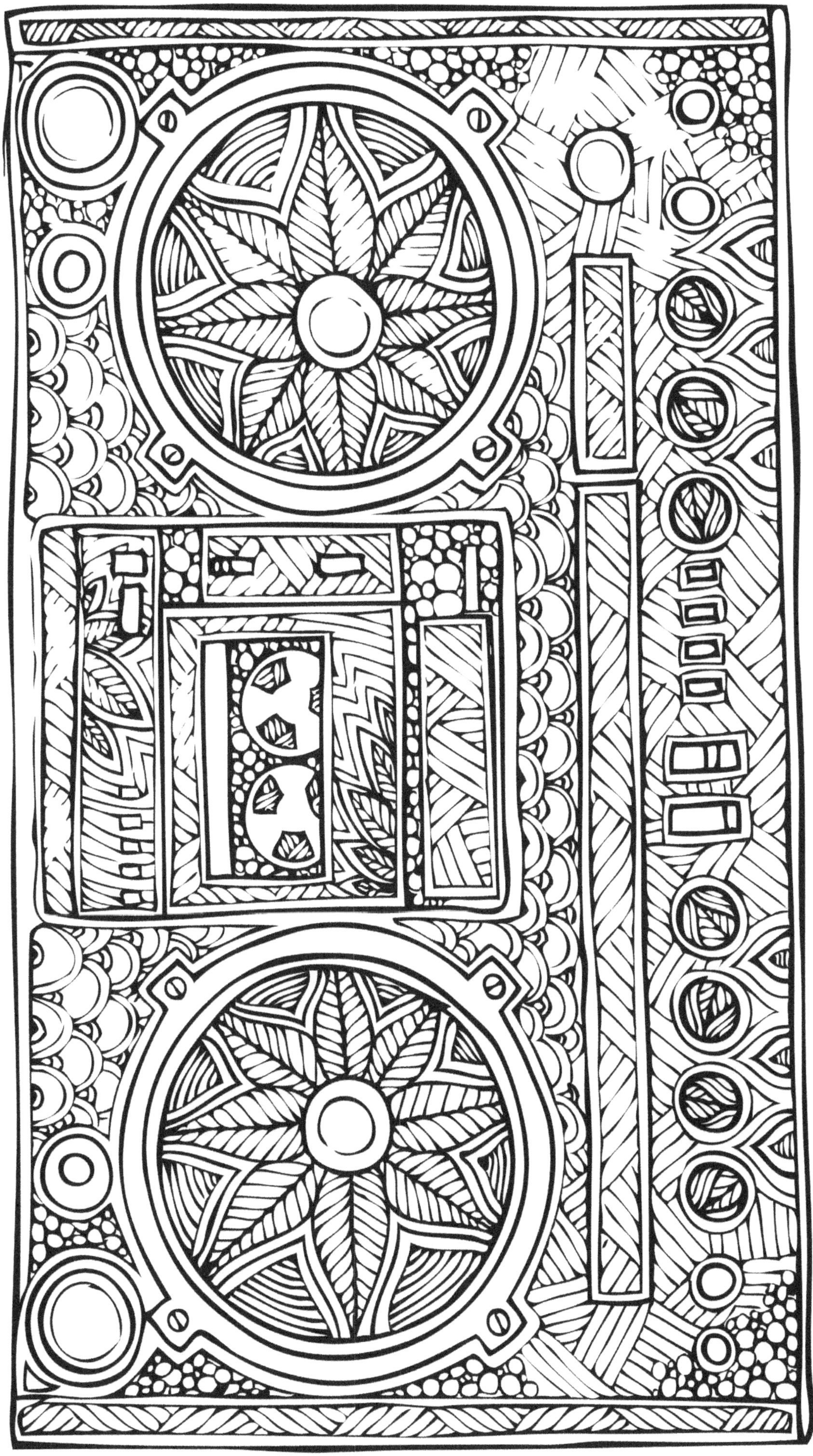

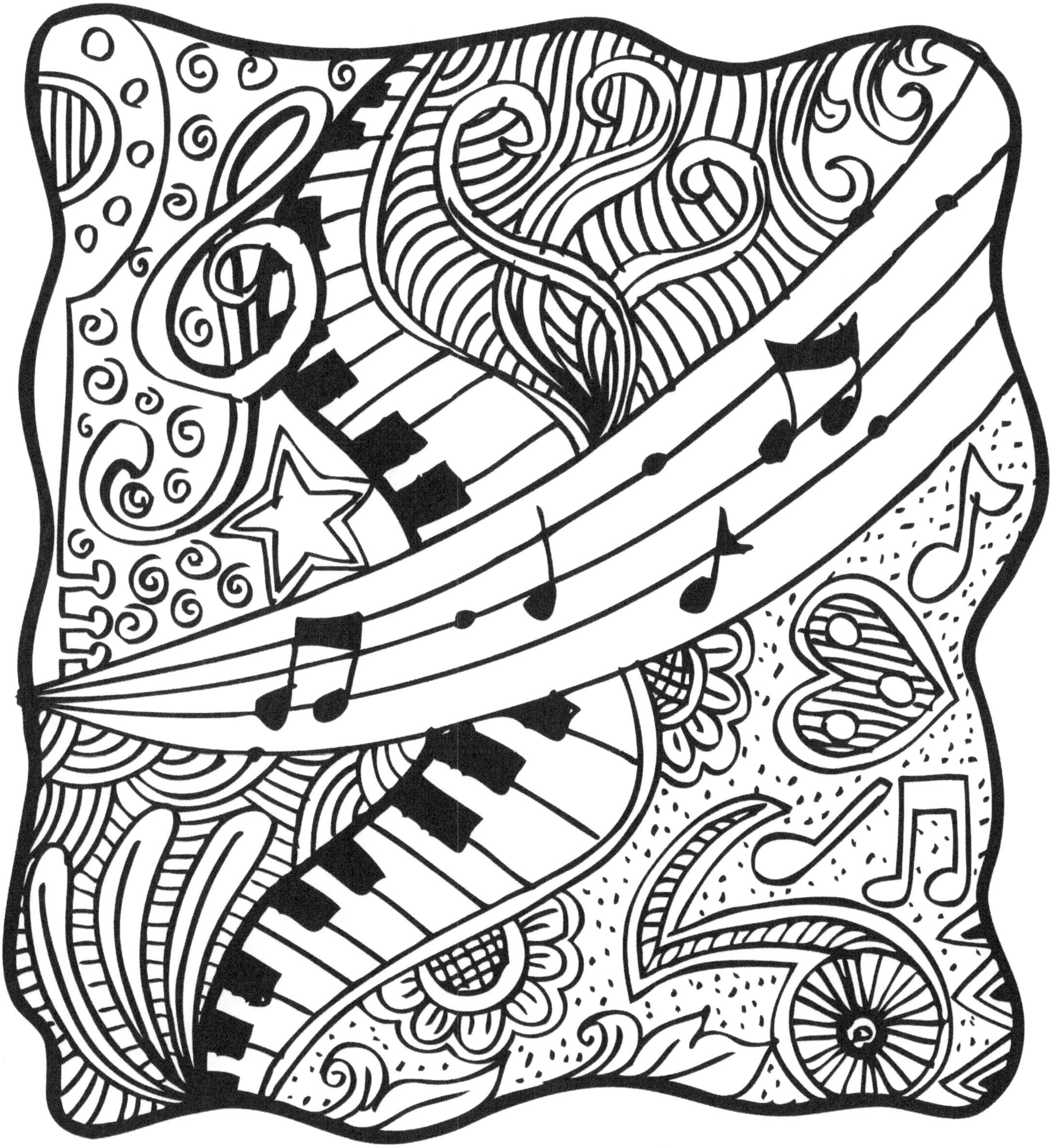

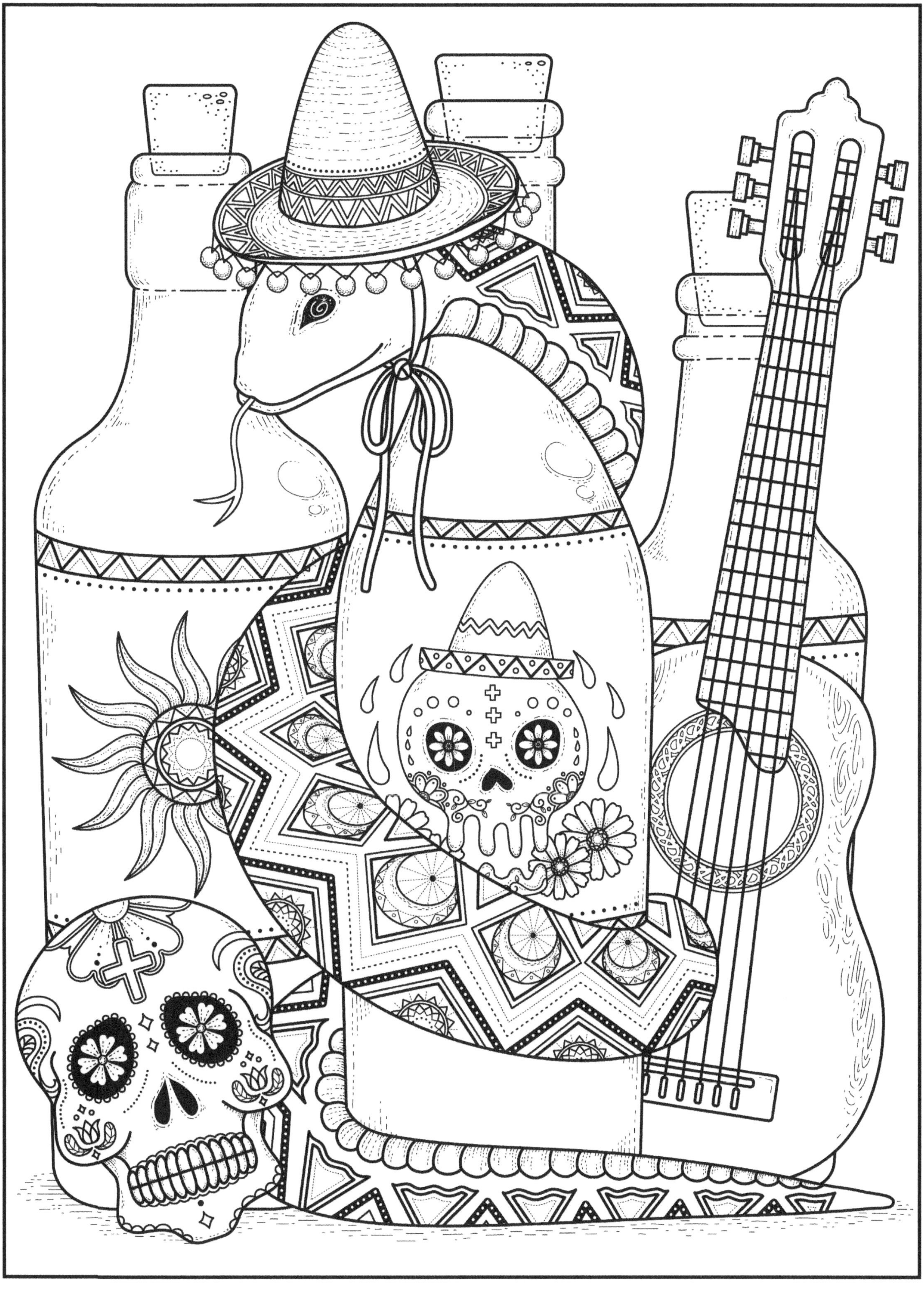

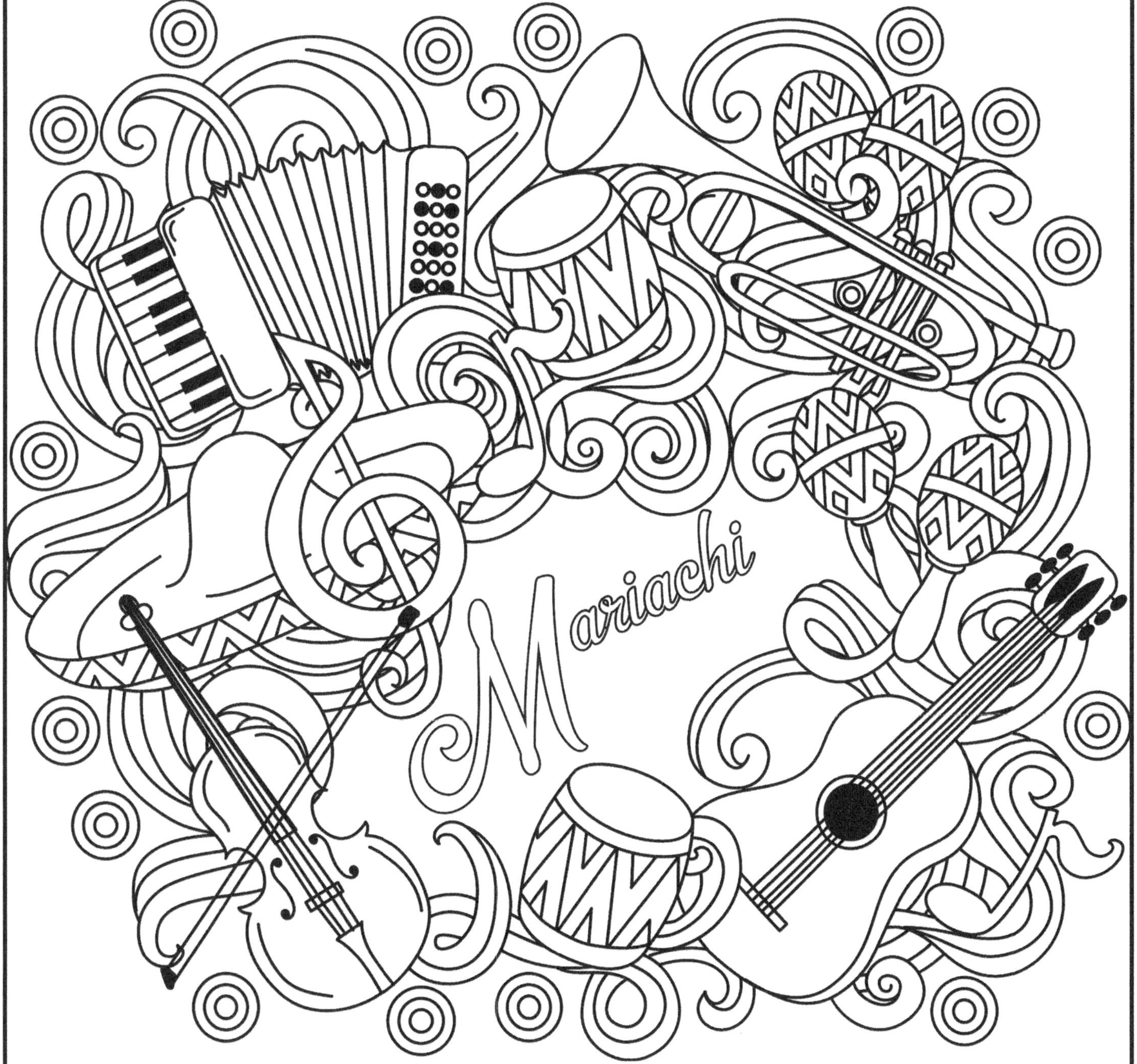
Mariachi

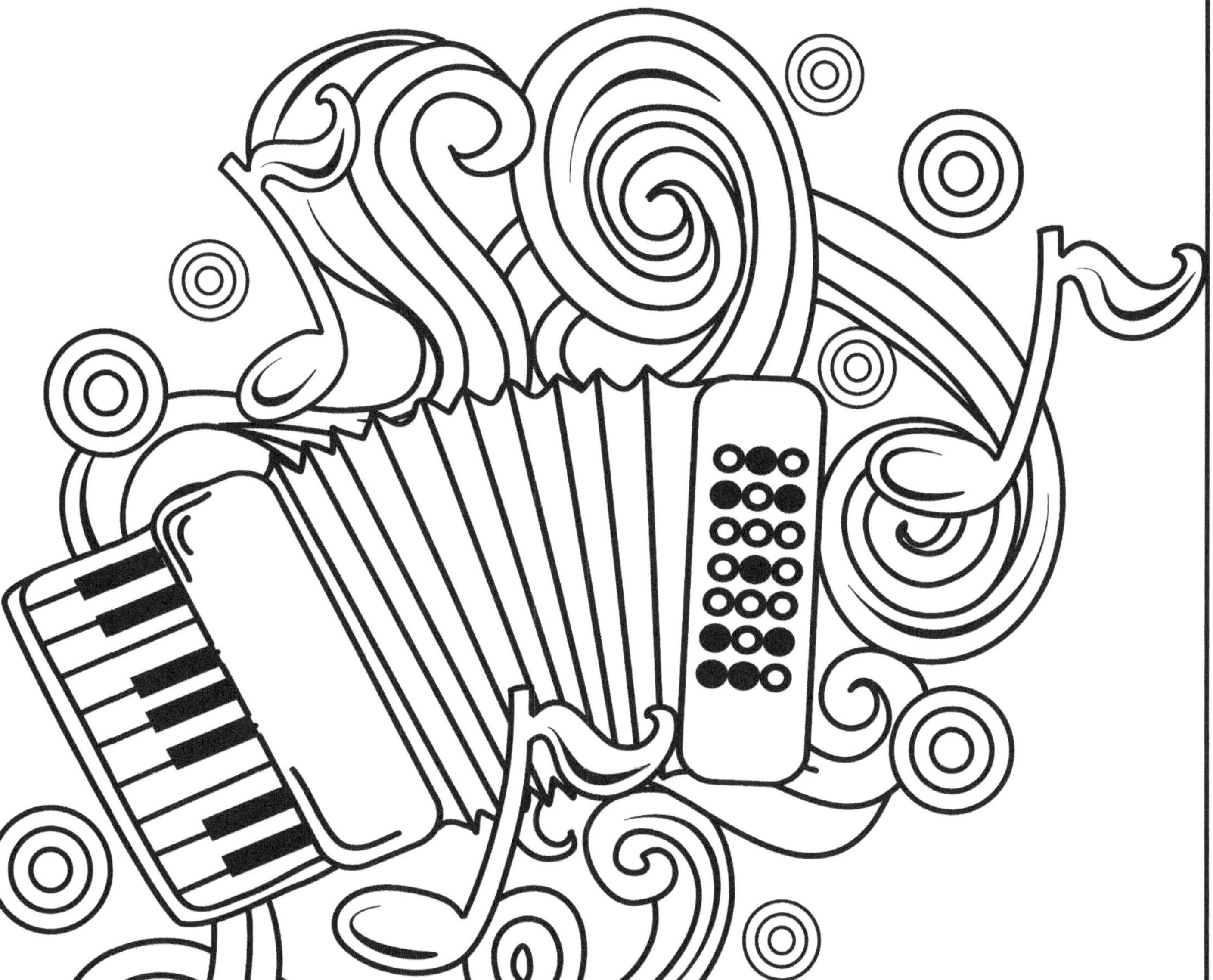

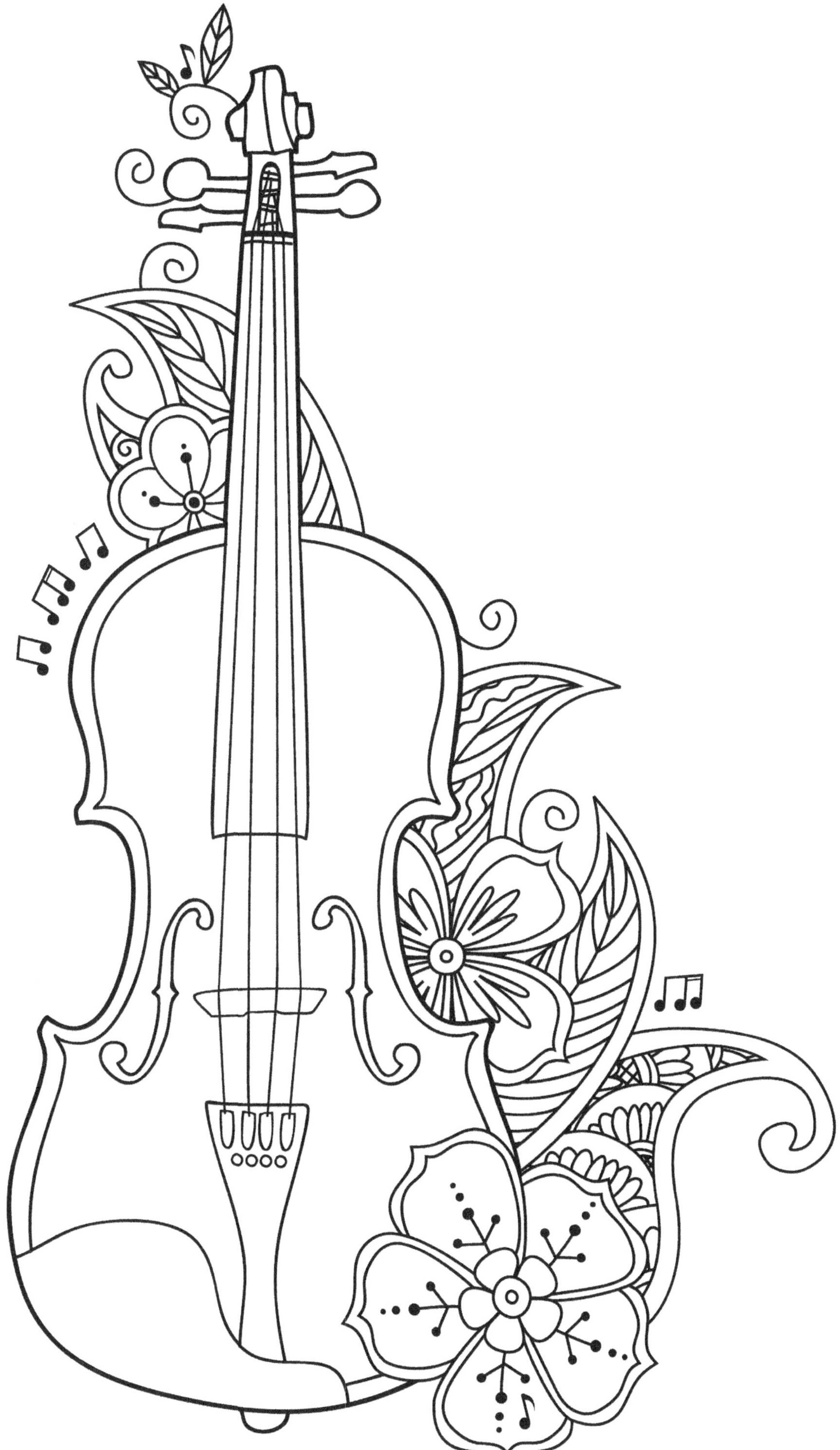

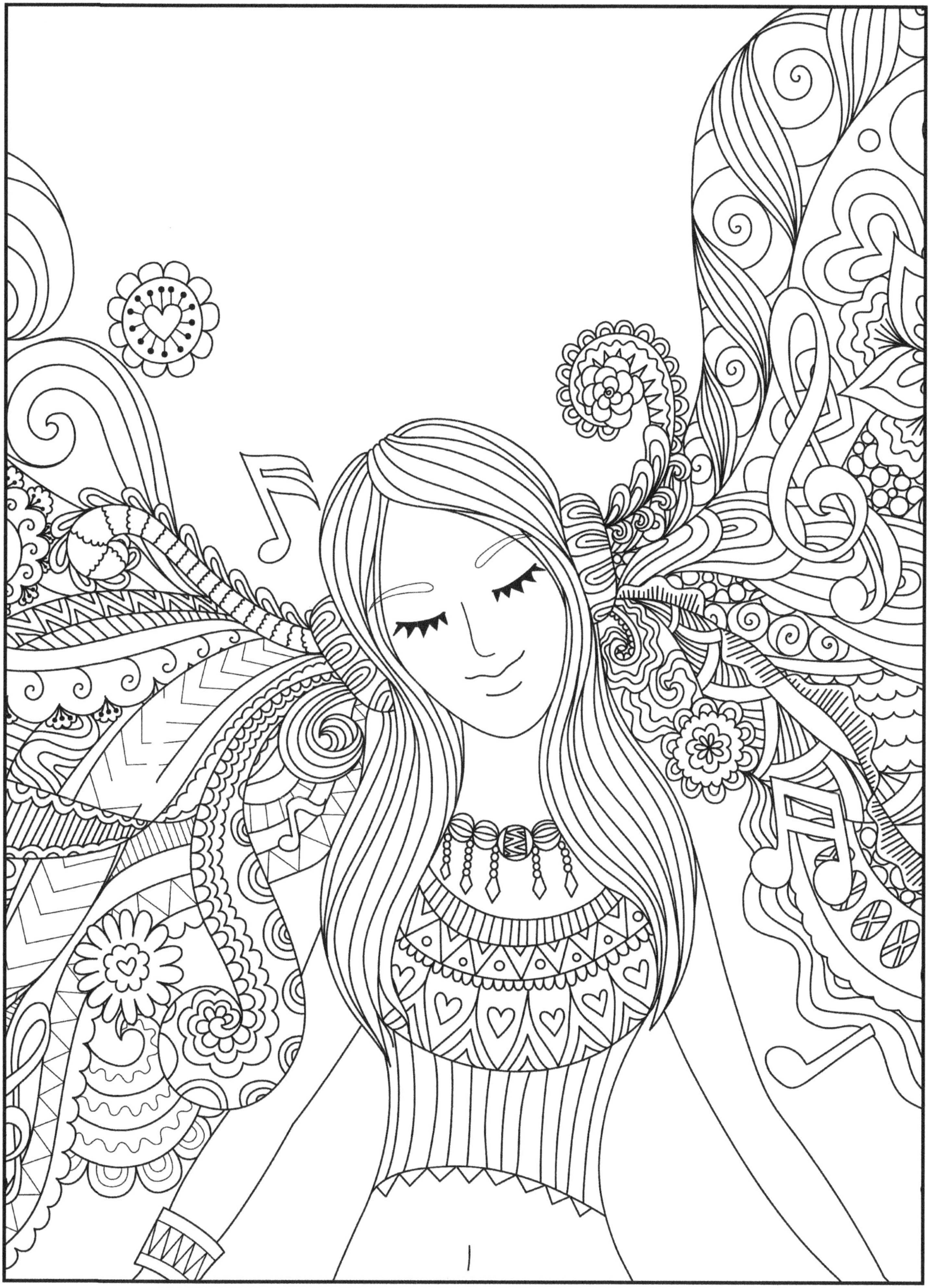

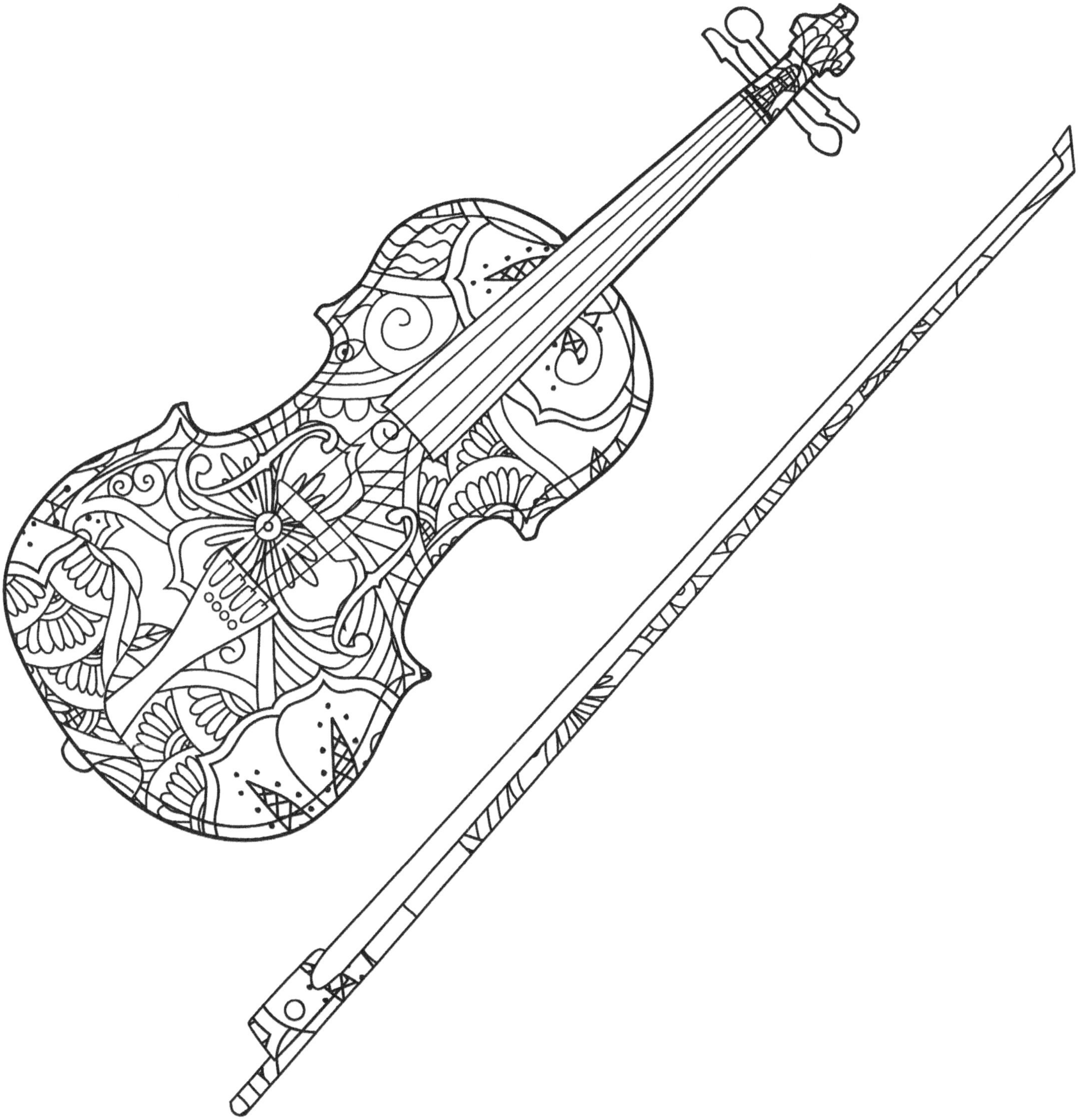

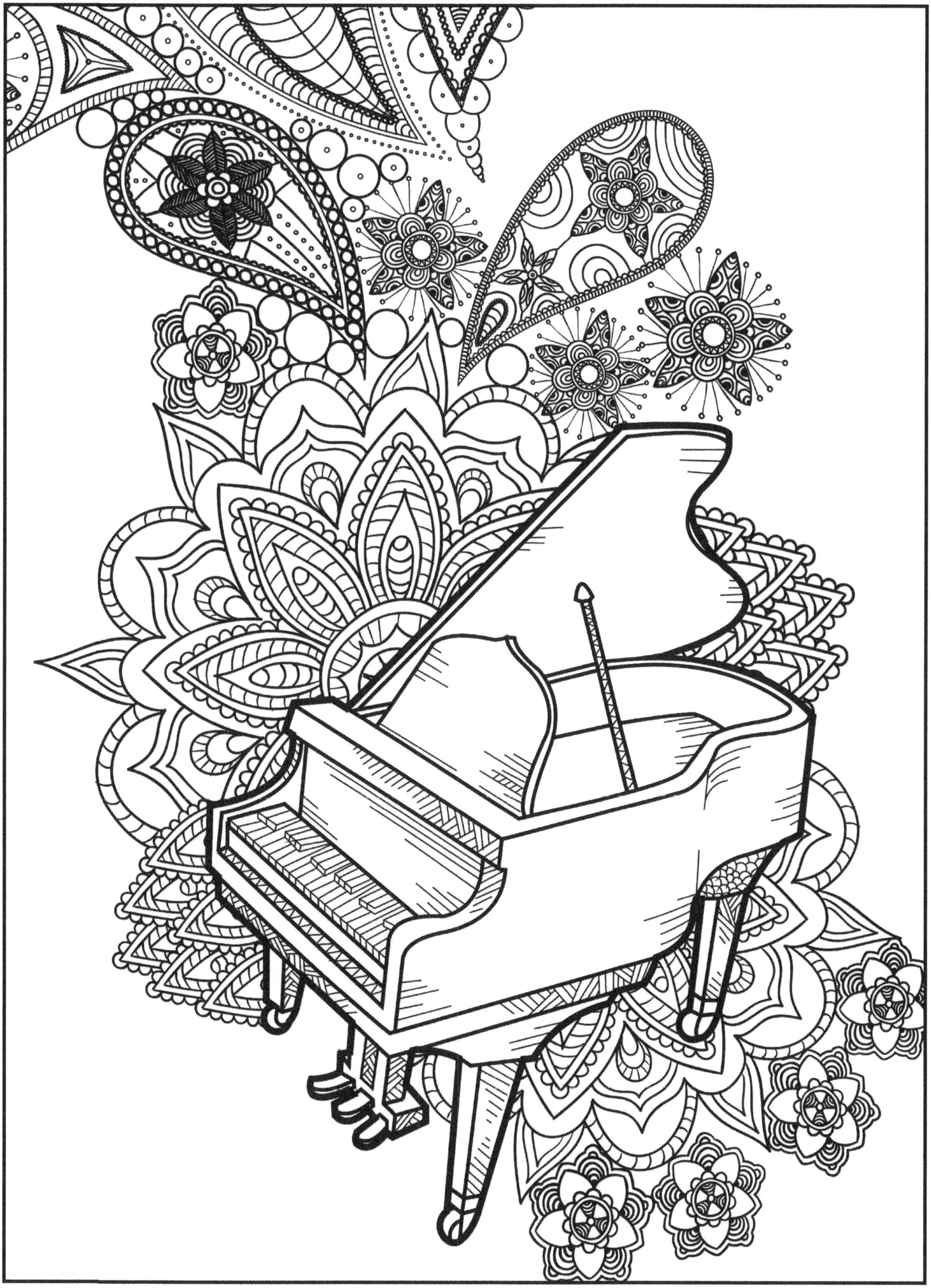

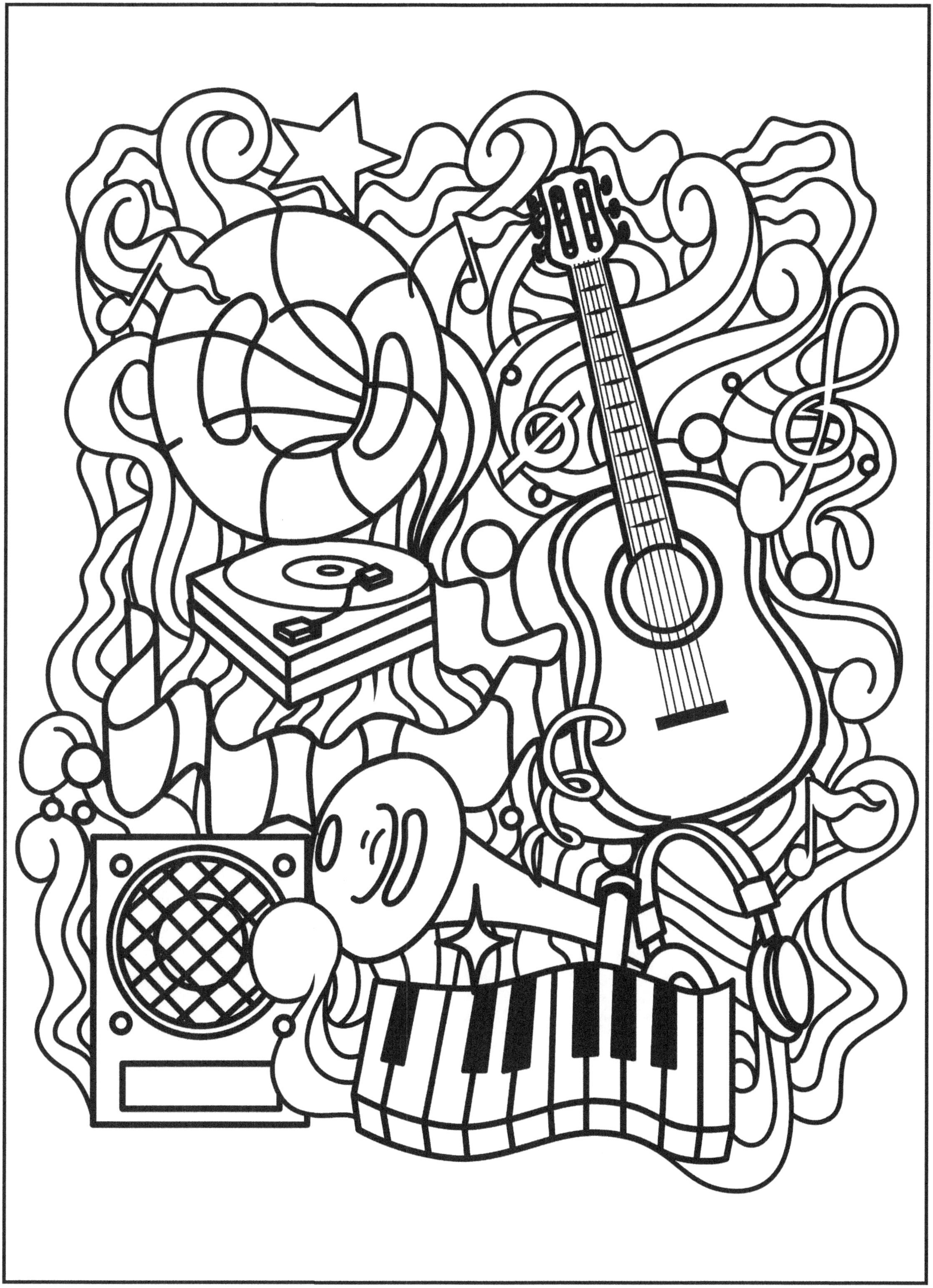

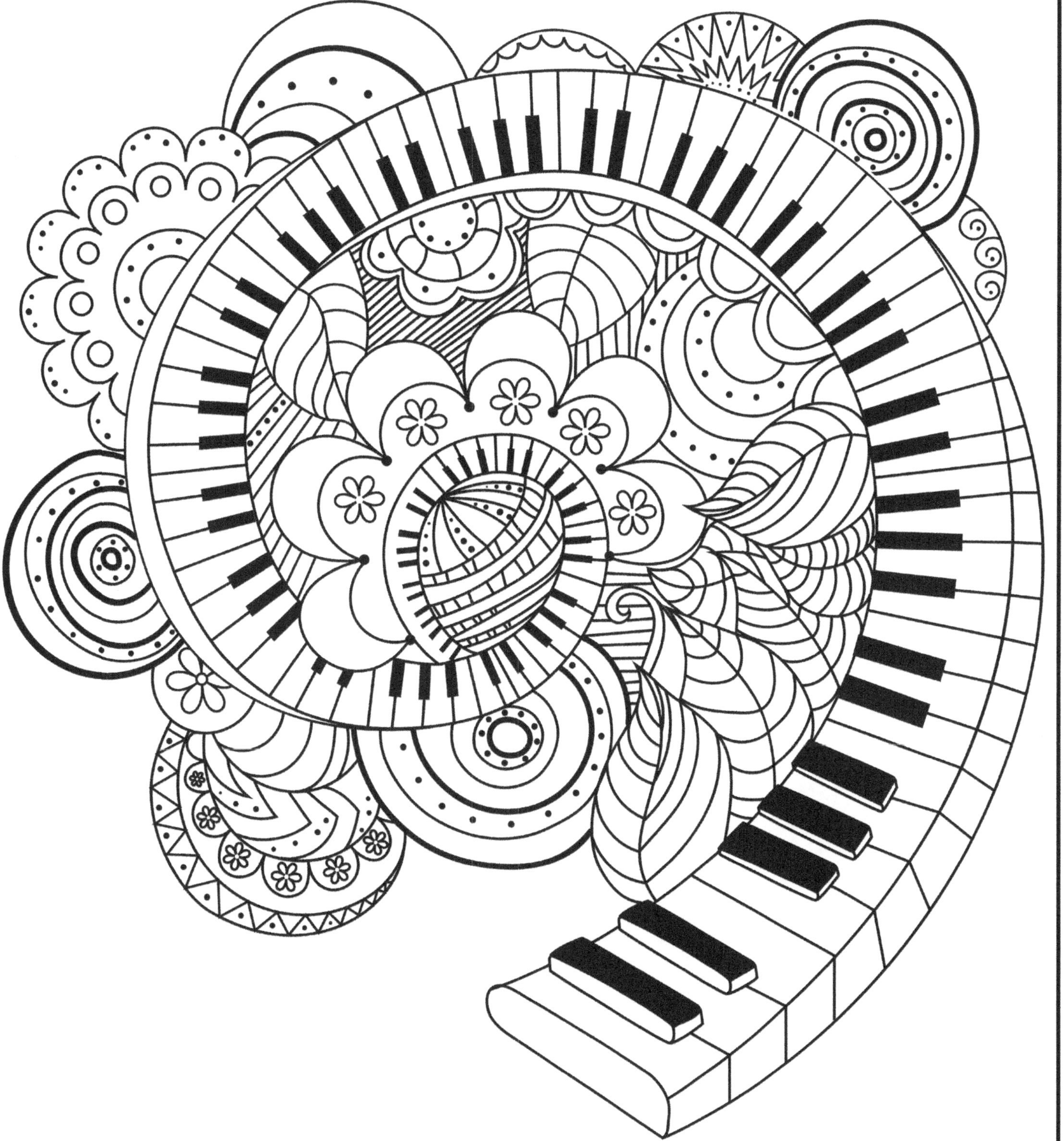

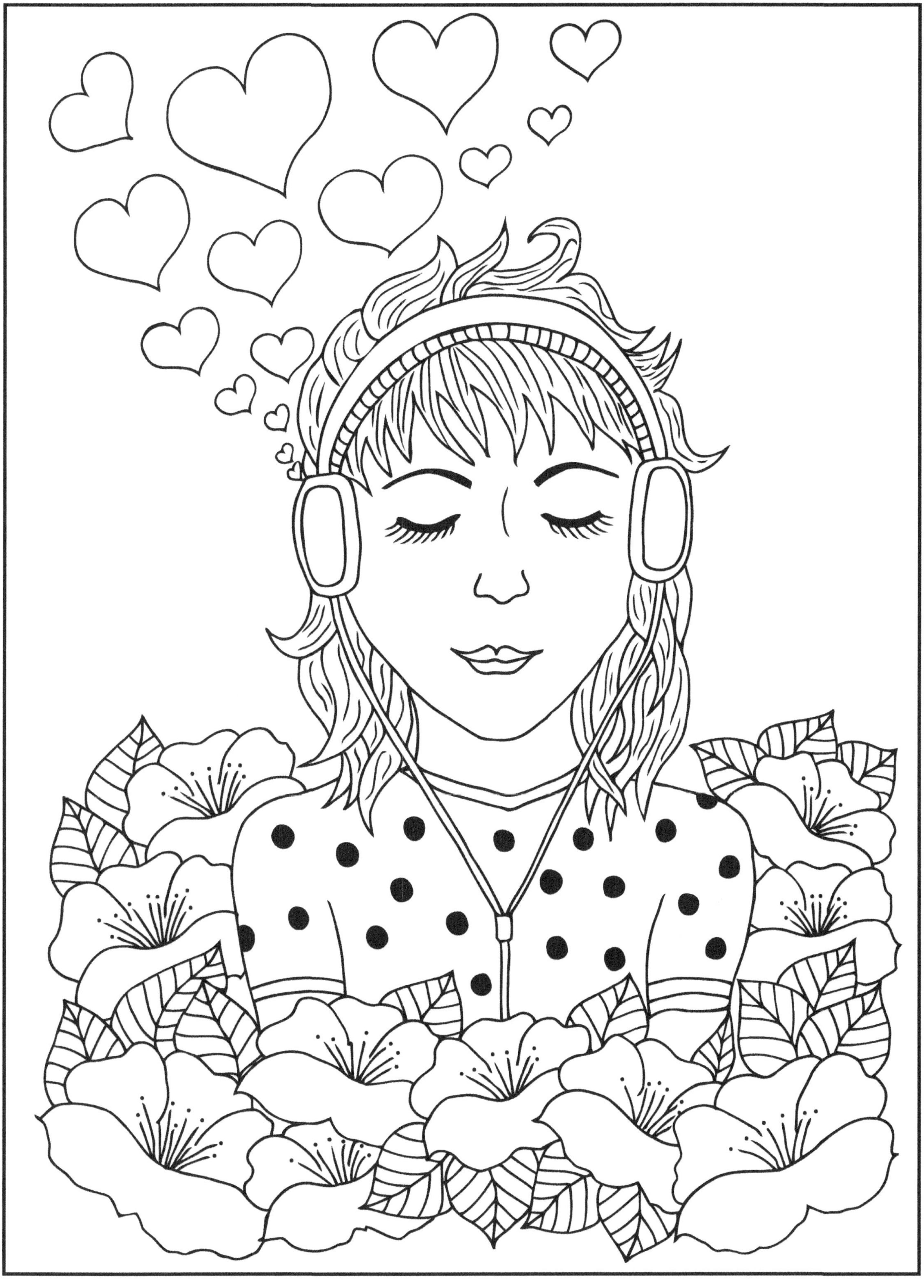

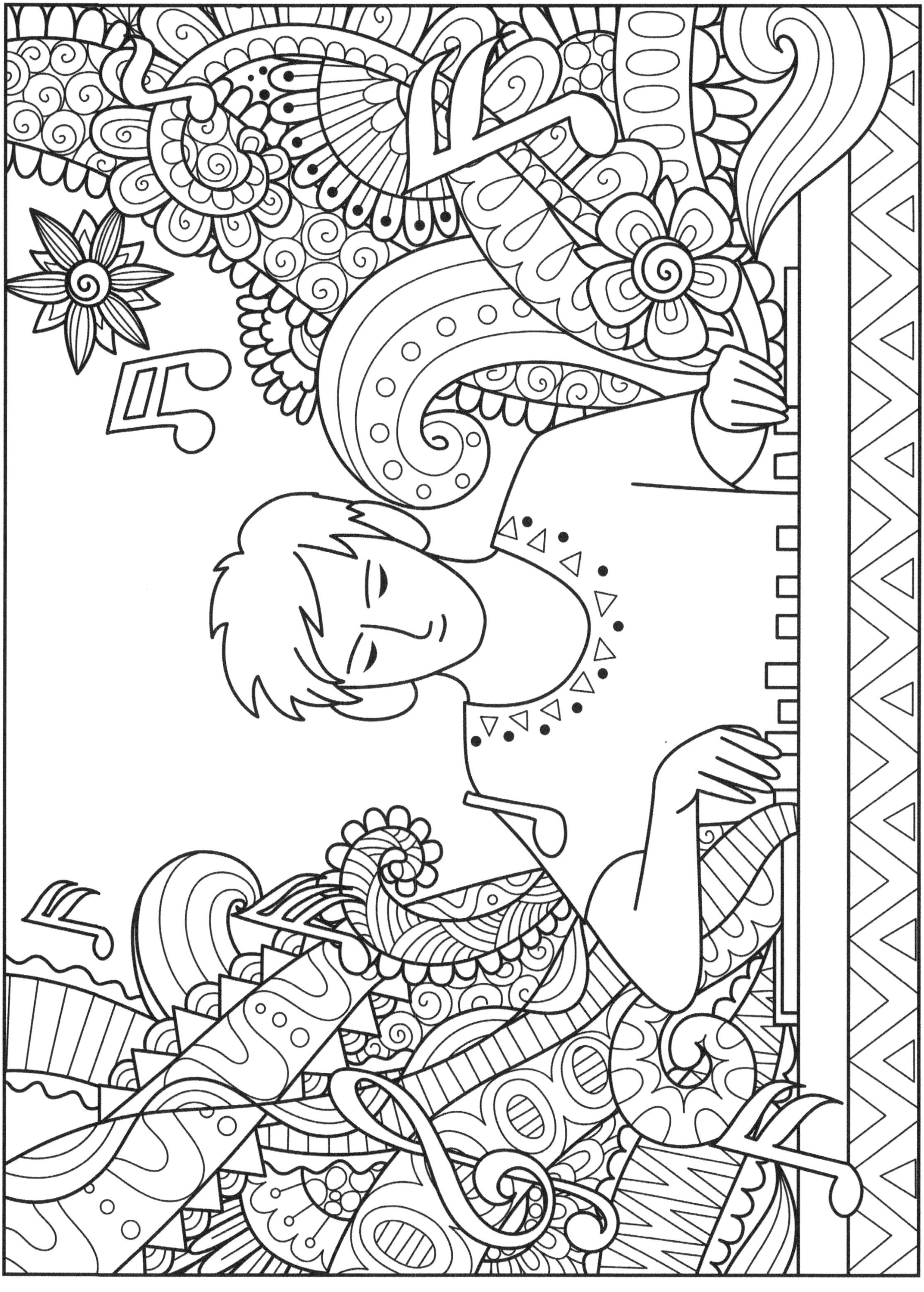

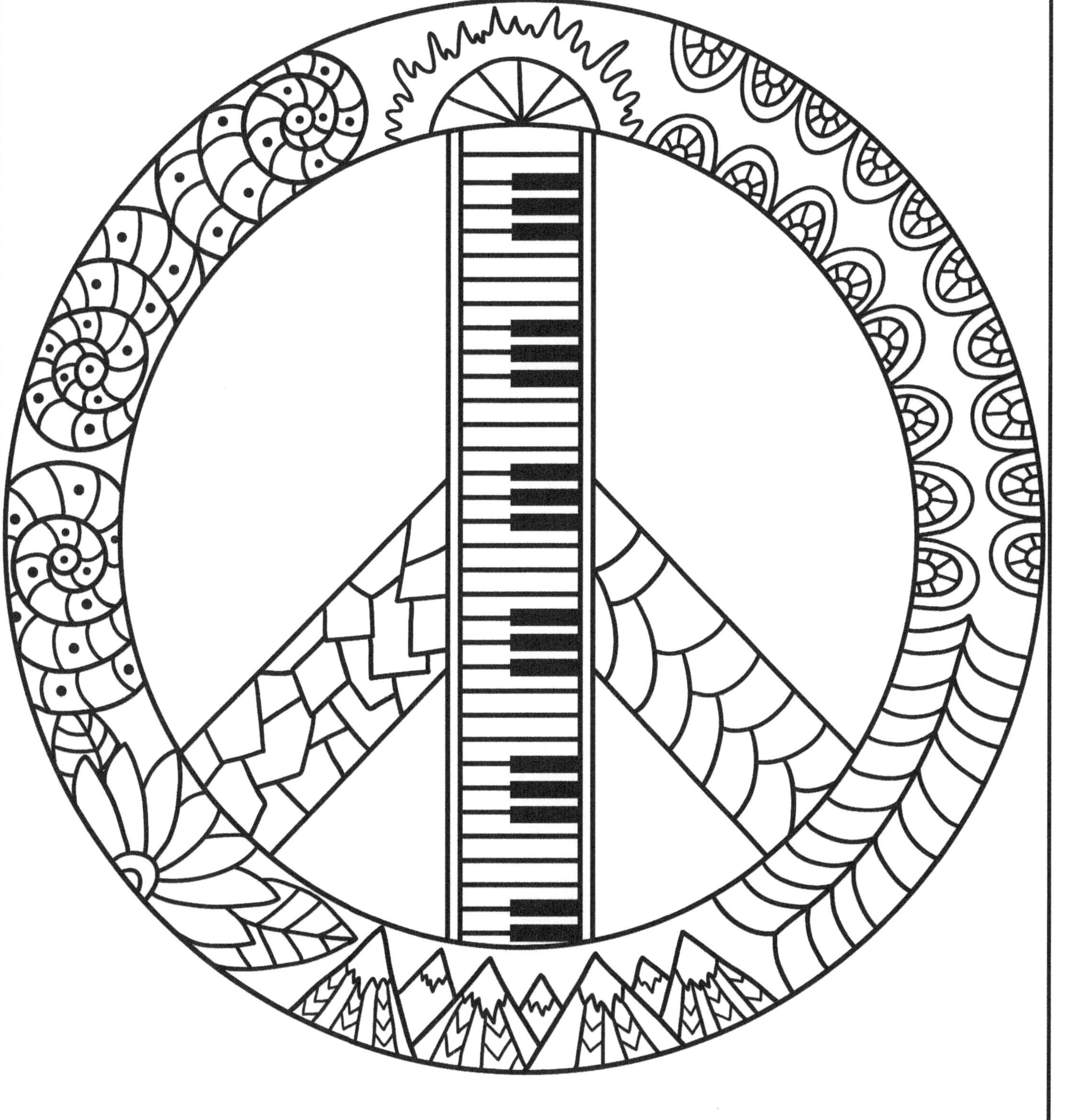

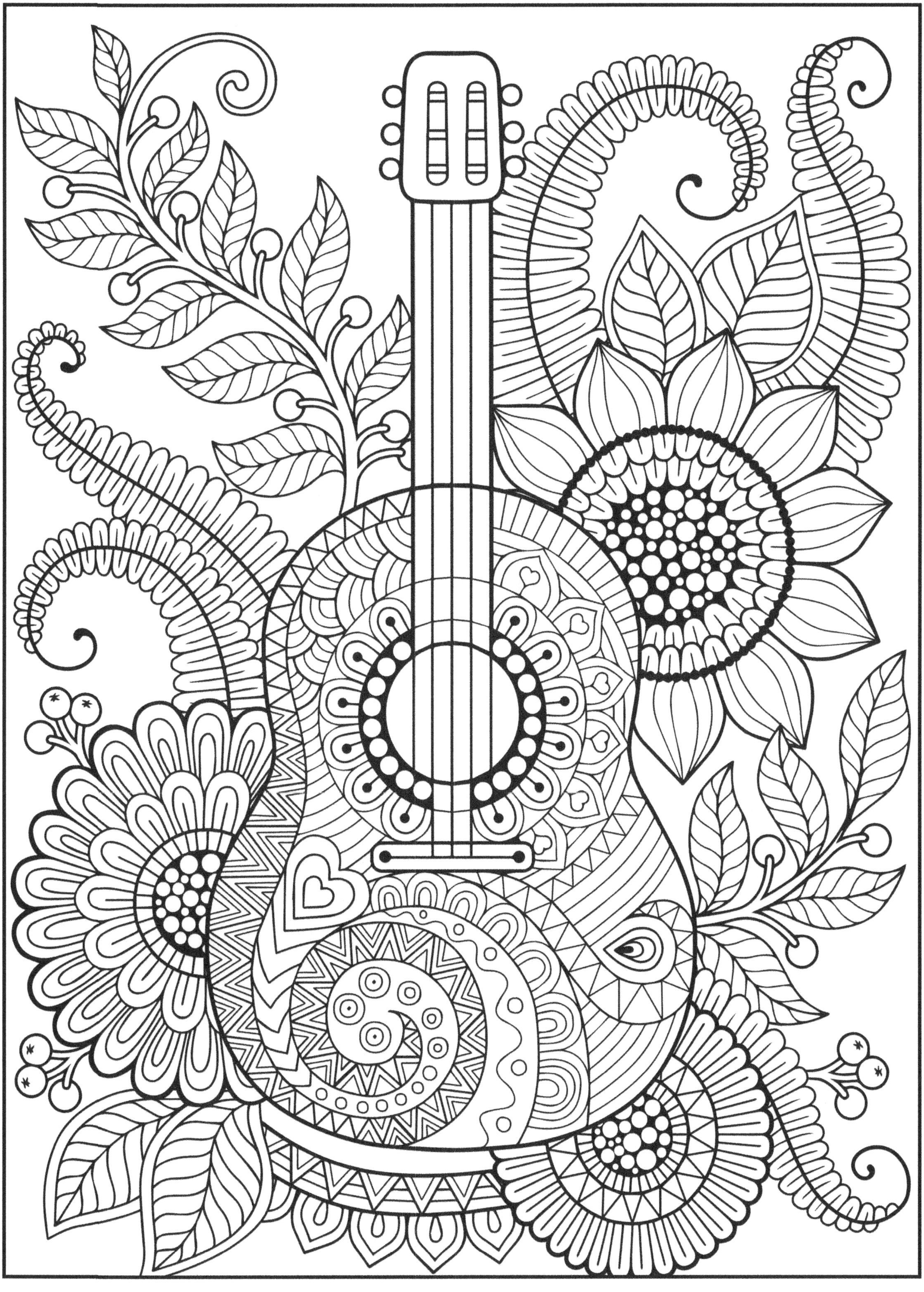

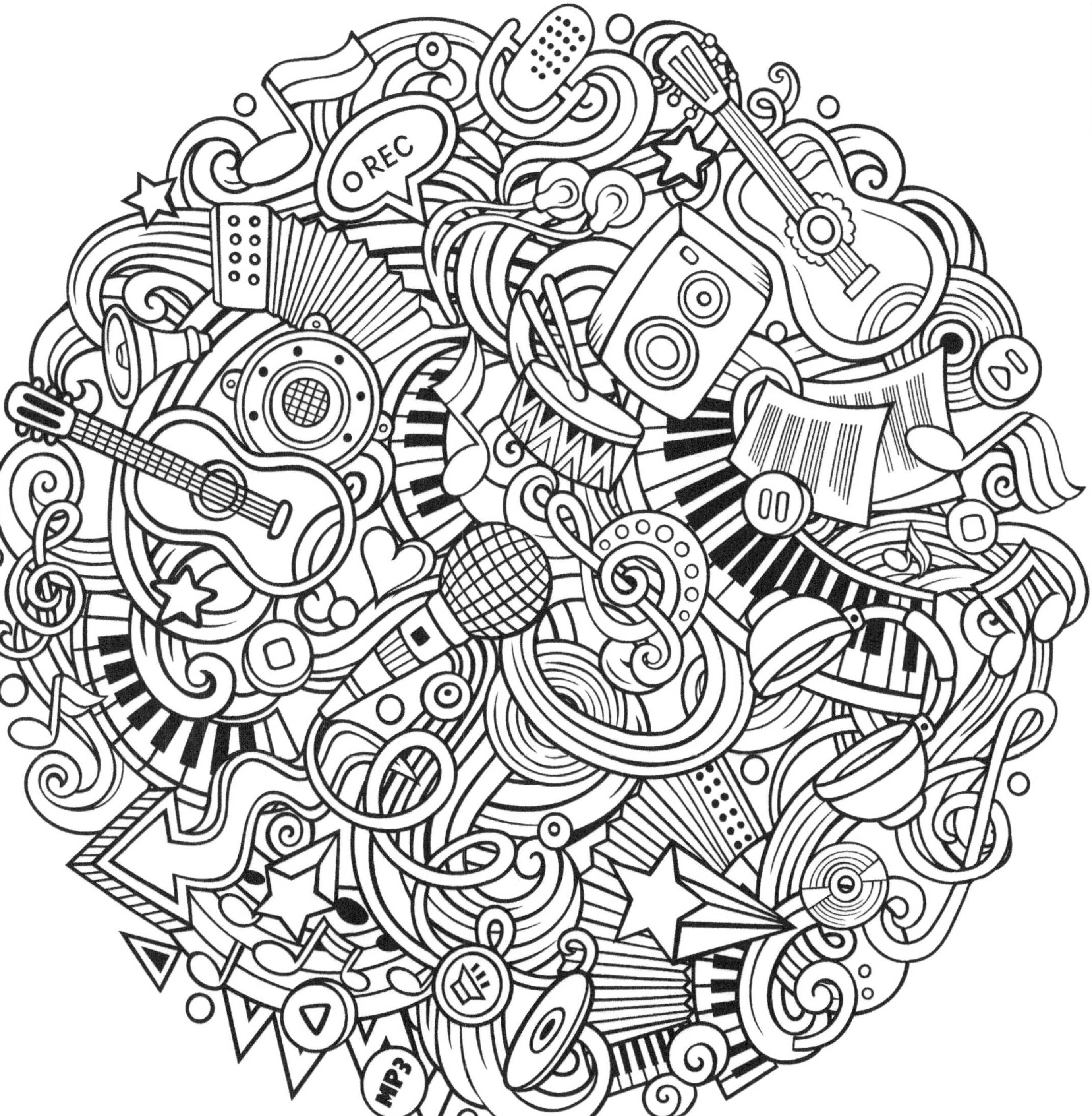

REC
MP3

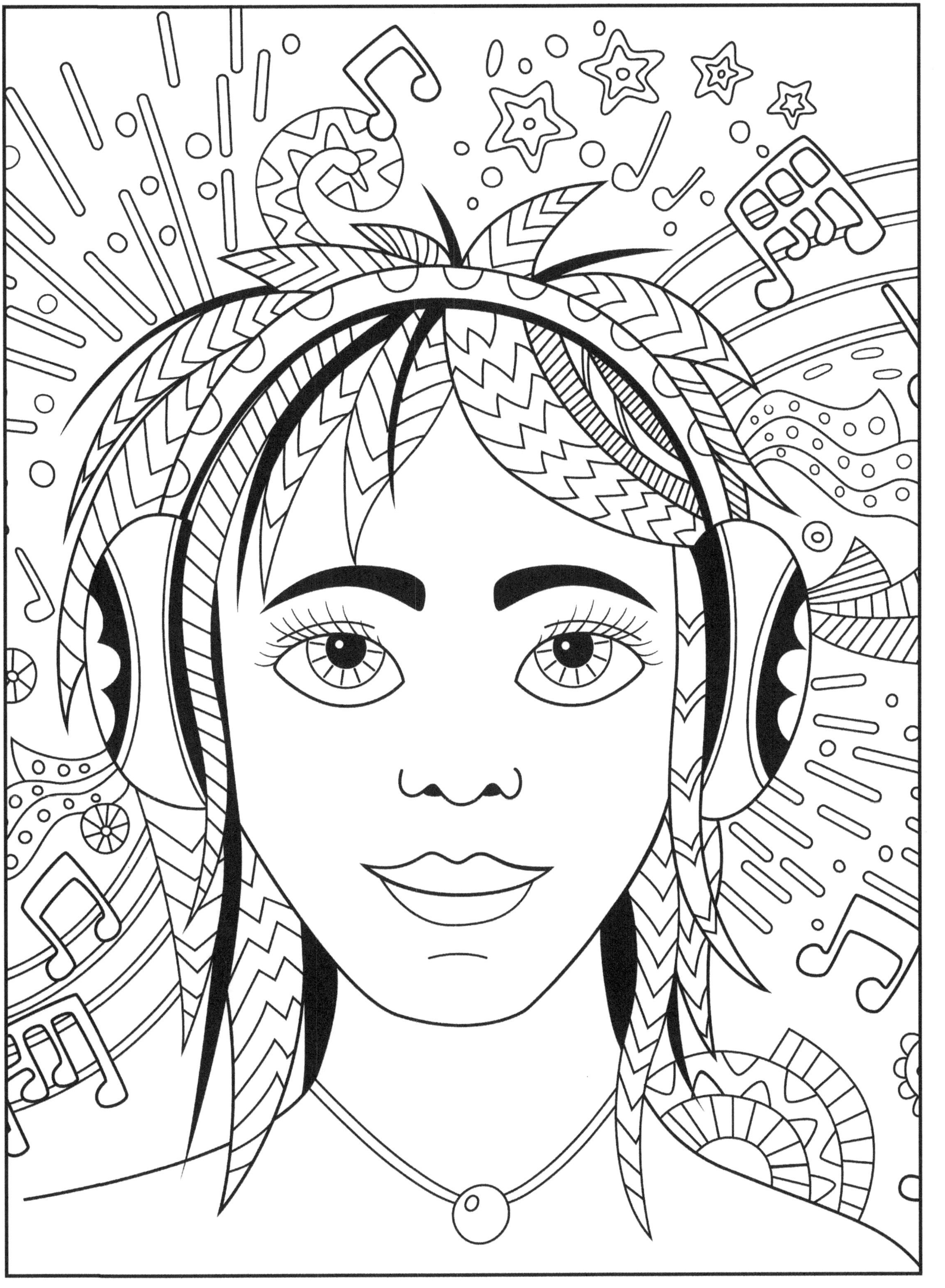

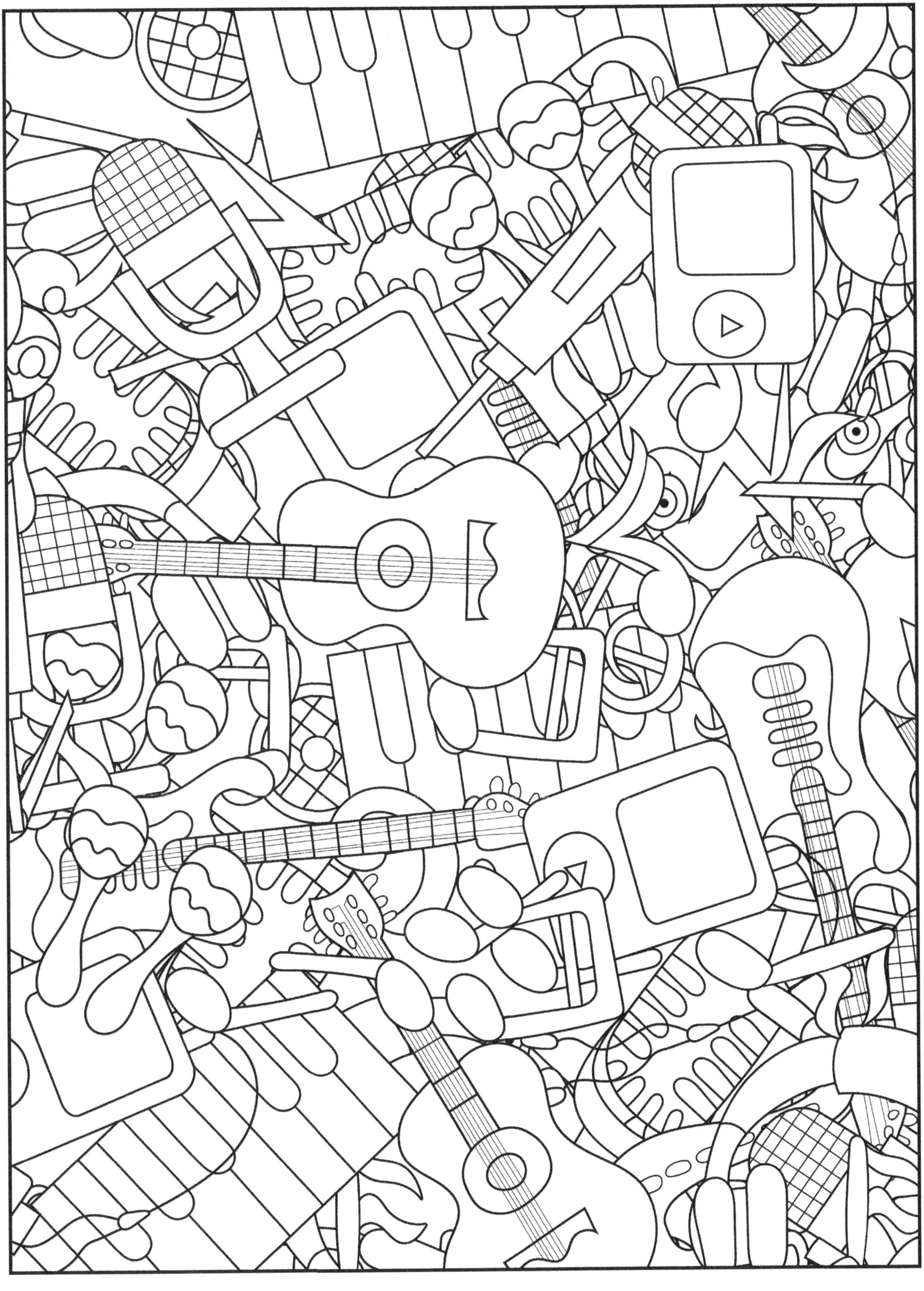

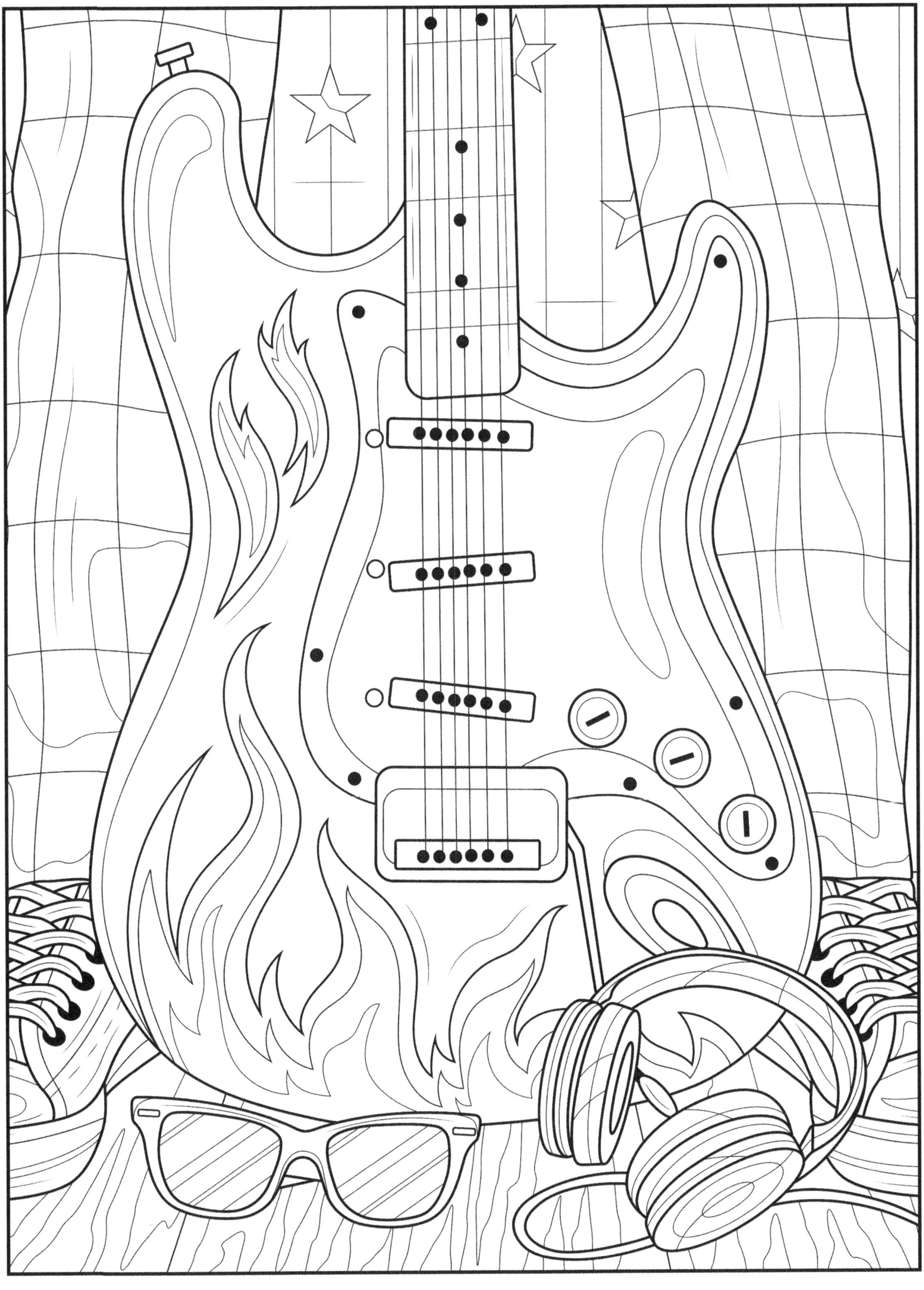

Made in the USA
Monee, IL
24 May 2022

96978279R00057